PROMISCUOUS CUSTOMERS:
INVISIBLE BRANDS

MICHAEL BAYLER AND DAVID STOUGHTON

PROMISCUOUS CUSTOMERS: INVISIBLE BRANDS

DELIVERING VALUE IN DIGITAL MARKETS

CAPSTONE

The right of Michael Bayler and David Stoughton to be identified as the authors of this
work has been asserted in accordance with the Copyright, Designs and Patents Act 1988.

First published 2002 by
Capstone Publishing (a Wiley company)
8 Newtec Place
Magdalen Road
Oxford OX4 1RE
United Kingdom
http://www.capstone.co.uk

British Library Cataloguing in Publication Data
A CIP catalogue record for this book is available from the British Library.

ISBN 1-84112-159-2

Typeset in 11/16 pt Palatino by
Sparks Computer Solutions Ltd, Oxford
http://www.sparks.co.uk
Printed and bound by
T.J. International Ltd, Padstow, Cornwall

This book is printed on acid-free paper

Substantial discounts on bulk quantities of Capstone books are available to
corporations, professional associations and other organisations. For details
telephone Capstone Publishing on (+44-1865-798623), fax (+44-1865-240941)
or email (info@wiley-capstone.co.uk).

To our families, of course, with love.

Contents

Acknowledgements

As always, many people contributed both directly and indirectly to this book. Thanks to all of you. In particular we'd like to mention Mark Allin and Richard Burton of Capstone, who started all this and then put up with the consequences!

Individually, Mike would like to thank Richard Gill, Tom Logan, Mark Middleton and, especially, Jane Roberts. David would like to thank David Thunder, Dev Sen, Rowan Jackson, Paul Owens and Umi Sinha.

Is This Book for You?

If you looked at the cover before turning to this page, and more or less liked what you saw, then almost certainly yes ...

All sorts of people, all over the world, with a wide variety of job descriptions and titles, are battling with the issue of how to – how shall we put it – 'do the right thing' in digital media. Consultants like us, board directors, strategists of all kinds, academics, Web designers, brand managers and all sorts of marketing folk, IT managers, software developers. And so on.

Let's cut to the chase ... if you're interested in what happens next with customers, businesses and their brands, the Internet, e-business, e-commerce and m-commerce, and all the rest, we wrote this book for you. We think it frames the most important questions at the time of writing,[1] and that it goes a long way towards answering a lot of them.

NOTES

1   Summer 2001.

Introduction

There was no 'One, two, three, and away!', but they began running when they liked, and left off when they liked, so that it was not easy to know when the race was over. However, when they had been running half an hour or so, and were quite dry again the Dodo suddenly called out 'The race is over!' and they all crowded round it panting, and asking 'But who has won?'.

A CHANGE OF DIRECTION

A bit of honesty ... We set out writing this book with the perhaps jaded hope that some of our more successful (and well-worn!) consulting tools and techniques might find a useful resting place in print. We'd struggled individually and together as a partnership for more years than we'd like to admit to (more than 20 years combined, if you must know ...) with the issue of what constitutes genuine value for customers – and therefore delivers value to businesses – in the digital domain. So we felt we had plenty to say, a thoroughly tested conceptual framework and vocabulary, and lots of real case materials to support our arguments.

A piece of cake, in other words.

But as we moved into the always challenging – *caveat emptor!* – and occasionally excruciating process of, well, doing the work rather than simply talking about it, we realised that (a) we couldn't just cynically regurgitate old thinking of our own and do justice either to our own efforts or to your invested time; and (b) we'd die of boredom.

But most importantly, we discovered very early in the process that far from just helping clients and readers make the most of the current digital environment, we needed to point out that this environment is in fact fatally flawed in terms of its ability to create substantial and sustainable value for either customer or business.

After some pretty serious discussion, we decided to dig a little deeper into the murky worlds of our combined experience, to develop what we believe to be a viable strategic stance and toolkit to meet this considerable challenge. We proceeded to explore how the implications of this thinking might actually play out in the future of digital markets.[1]

As a consequence, we believe that we've come up with a clear overview of what the next convincing manifestation of digital business will look like. Internet 3? Perhaps.

Anyway … hard work! Not what we'd envisaged.

But we're happy with the fruits of this unanticipated labour, and we encourage you to engage with these observations, conclusions and recommendations with an open and critical mind. Disagree with us, heap scorn on our efforts. But most of all, move forward, and take nothing for granted. Lots of changes are afoot, as you'll see below, and they will demand both open minds and enormous effort from those of us looking to participate.

Whatever this thing is, it's clearly only now getting under way. *Bon voyage!*

AFTER THE FALL ...

Obviously, despite the recent dip in the technology markets, digital media remain set for extraordinary growth. ActivMedia, for example (Fig. 0.1), puts the total value of Internet-generated revenue by 2002 at $US 1234 billion, while Forrester (Fig. 0.2) puts US e-commerce (in this case probably e-business) at $US 1331 billion by 2003.

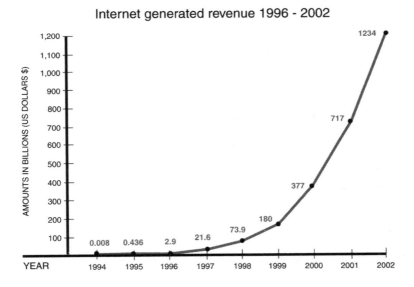

Fig. 0.1 By 2002, the overall size of the digital business opportunity hits – according to ActivMedia – a staggering $US 1234 billion.[2]

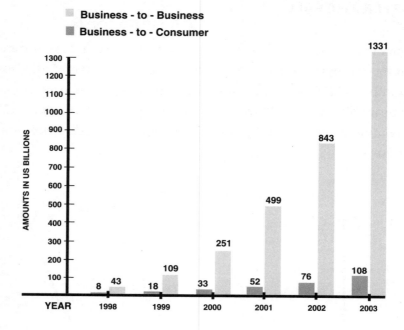

US ECOMMERCE 1998 - 2003

Business - to - Business
Business - to - Consumer

Fig. 0.2 Forrester Research are similarly bullish in their predictions, but note also the difference in scale between their B2B and B2C estimates.[3]

But it's equally clear that all is not entirely well. As we'll see below, help is urgently needed on both the demand and supply sides.

Customers are not at all happy with on-line businesses ...

In September 2000, A.T. Kearney, an EDS division, conducted research into experienced on-line consumers' behaviour in six of the most developed digital markets: the US, UK, Sweden, Germany, France and Japan (representing 89% of the (then) worldwide market).[4]

The report conveyed this dismaying news:

' ... e-retailers are missing out on more than $6.1 billion in lost sales today, or 13% of the total worldwide revenue. If e-retailers do not get their act together, they will never reach predicted forecasts. The main reason for this missed opportunity is that consumers cannot do what they want on-line ... If e-retailers wish to satisfy the demands of customers, they must first offer them *an on-line experience that meets expectations.*' (Our italics.)

... businesses are not at all happy with their suppliers ...

A 2001 report from Elmwood[5] presents equally dismal news for players on the supply side, in particular the marketing services sector. Fully 30% of clients indicate that they do not intend to use their previous agency again. A further 30% would not recommend them to another client.

Why is this the case? Well, another report, from the Henley Centre,[6] places lack of support for business process by agencies among the most serious problems for clients and, looking at both reports, we can see the dramatic contrast between technology-based complaints (a mere 14%) and failure to deliver on an operational or other component (61%).

... and nobody's happy about losing so much money!

No need to detail the woeful list of losers in the dot-com frenzy. Less newsworthy perhaps, but also far more alarming, is the statistic we uncovered in our recent research into production processes in the UK digital market. Some 20% of projects are making a profit on the supply side, with the rest losing money.

GartnerGroup anticipated this issue two years ago:[7]

'Through 2002 GartnerGroup gives 75% of e-business projects a 50–50 chance of meeting their objectives. The main reason? *Fundamental flaws in strategic preparation and project management.'*(Our italics)

WAKE-UP CALLS FROM THE RECENT PAST

The point needs to be made here that the various industries that converge in digital media – as well as their clients – have repeatedly insisted on misreading the strategic opportunities afforded by the new media, the slow-motion explosion of the supporting technologies, their implementation and their (generally grudging and unpredictable) acceptance by customers.

At least three consistent strategic distractions still persist in exerting a savage downward pull on the trajectory of digital markets. What's most alarming, in terms of the argument of this book as well as the prospects for digital markets overall, is that their negative effects have been demonstrated clearly, repeatedly and at enormous cost over the past ten years. Both the early interactive revolution – where compact disc was the primary vehicle – and the subsequent Internet explosion of the mid-to-late 90s, were blighted in varying degrees by an over-focus upon them.

Now, eerily, the same mantras are heard at the time of writing this (although less lustily chanted than in the golden months of mad investment) around the halls of digital media, as the focus – rightly or wrongly, certainly shakily – moves from the Web to Interactive TV, broadband and 3G mobile.

The question is now, when will we choose to wake up? Will we wake up at all?

The obsession with bandwidth

Bandwidth – its lack, the need for more, how wonderful it'll be then, and so on – has occupied centre stage since the early days of new media, and has perhaps taken over from processing power as 'the only thing that stands in our way'.

But what actually changes when, for example, broadband delivery to business and home becomes a reality? Beyond enabling a certain amount of convergence of delivery, beyond cutting download times for data, and beyond shifting the competitive environment around (again), in what circumstances does higher bandwidth create genuine new revenue streams? Is any meaningful new value delivered to businesses and consumers?

This is not to say that bandwidth does not enable new types of value to be created and delivered to customers, and correspondingly, new revenue streams to evolve for certain business models. But this is not the same thing as creating that value. We cannot continue to make the mistake of assuming – as has been the case with content – that more bandwidth automatically means more value. It's not true, and it leads to misdirected strategic efforts at the most fundamental levels.

The obsession with content

The profound misreading of the true value of content in digital markets is brought in here to back up our point about bandwidth, but is explored in detail in Chapter 5, 'Meaning, Trust and Value'. Surely only owners of media-rich content (audio and video primarily), which needs big pipelines for satisfactory delivery to the customer, and the owners of these pipelines, stand to benefit at all from this 'bulk' mentality. This is the idea that somehow, for the customer as well as the business, 'more is more'.

As long as 'content is king' remains on the lips of those who drive opportunities in digital markets, in the absence of a modally-based[8] approach that enables content to support – as opposed to impede – meaning, trust and value, the customer's core needs will continually fail to be met with, as we shall see later, commercially disastrous results.

The obsession with new channels and devices

At the time of writing, two major global manufacturers of consumer electronic goods – notably mobile phones and PDAs – are announcing huge lay-offs in their workforces.

While this is due in part to the general current cooling of the world economy, especially notable in technology stocks, it also reflects a new – and to a considerable extent justified – uncertainty about the hitherto rosy prospects of the 'mobile Internet'. The markets have furthermore, after a brief honeymoon period, thrown into question the absurdly high cost of the European 3G mobile licences.

As for Interactive TV, while plenty of pilots continue to be run, the real opportunities become increasingly vague and, frankly, narrow, as the veneer of technical optimism wears thinner. TV – interactive or not – generally remains a resolutely passive medium, where the task-focused customer is unlikely to find adequate, coherent ways to solve problems, except of the very simplest kind. It seems that most of the more plausible interactive functions will develop around gaming-type options, and that the dryer applications relating to, for example, banking, will tend to stay rooted in more work-based channels.

Our points made above about the problems created by an over-focus on content and bandwidth are again relevant here. Outside a modal, truly customer-centric approach, where necessarily complex partnerships of complementary businesses are together able to provide a rich, complete experience to the customer, the obsession with new channels is little more than an expensive distraction. As with bandwidth, mistaking the potential enabler of value for the value itself has severe consequences.

OUR TEN PARADOXES IN DIGITAL MARKETS

There's a good reason why you'll find a quote from the work of

Lewis Carroll (*Alice in Wonderland* and *Through the Looking Glass*) at the head of each chapter in this book: any meaningful exploration of business in digital markets immediately uncovers mazes, riddles and irritations of all kinds. So Alice became our mascot, with her apparently inexhaustible curiosity, her courage, her humour and – perhaps the most necessary qualities of all in this generally hostile landscape – her determination and occasional bursts of anger.

Less frivolously, with the two key themes of meaning and trust running through *Promiscuous Customers*, what better source of inspiration for the enterprise than these masterpieces of wisdom and nonsense, friendships and betrayals, reality and fantasy?

We uncovered a number of fascinating riddles in the course of our work. These are the most impactful, and we have endeavoured to develop and answer them in the nine chapters that follow.

In digital markets, then …

1   Why is information, far from adding value, the cause of most of the problems encountered by customers and businesses? Why is content anything but king?

2   Why will the most important information never be seen by the very customers who are most willing to pay for it?

3   Why will tomorrow's most valuable brands be mostly invisible? And why is the 'virtual' or digital brand the realest brand we've ever had?

4   How can we manage brands that are intrinsically out of our control?

5   Why is Customer Relationship Management (CRM) in fact attacking value and destroying loyalty? What does it really mean to be customer-centric in an environment where loyalty is often meaningless?

6   How can customers be most loyal to the services of which they are least conscious? Why is mind share no longer relevant?

7   Why are the smallest and least significant aspects of the customer's digital experience the ones that put your business most at risk?

8   Why are today's e-commerce powerhouses tomorrow's low-end fulfilment houses?

9   Why is disintermediation in fact a blind alley, and partnership the only way forward for business?

10   Why is the analysis of the smallest customer task the only route to building sustainable business strategy?

HOW *PROMISCUOUS CUSTOMERS* IS PUT TOGETHER

A game of three halves ...

Here's the challenge we set ourselves in writing this book: how can we create sustainable value for businesses in digital markets, through the analysis and delivery of true value for their most valuable and desirable customers?

Our overall approach here has been to bring customer experience – for the first time we think (at least in earnest ...) – together with business strategy.

We look first at the problem in Chapters 1–3, broadly focusing upon the new customer, the new brand and the new business types that have emerged in recent years in digital markets. We find that meaning and trust are above all else the two key value drivers, and that ignoring these imperatives (as we see in Chapter 5) has taken digital media to some funny – or not so funny – places. We introduce a tool, the 'Revenue Cube', for the modelling of the key business types in the punishing and clearly unsustainable current environment that we dub the 'Commoditised Internet'.

We start the second of our three halves, by proposing and detailing at a high level, a new methodology for the discovery and description of customer value in digital markets, which we have named Modal Analysis. Working logically from the starting point of key customer tasks, Modal Analysis enables a business to evolve a truly value-based series of scenarios for the creation, delivery, and achievement of profit from its prospective digital offerings.

Our second key tool, the 'Cycles of Customer Experience', is usefully introduced here, enabling you to visualise how customers' individual perceptions and their individual experience can be managed forward, towards a new kind of 'digital loyalty' based upon cohesive task support and increasing automation of services.

Applying this methodology takes us in the direction of a completely new paradigm for the delivery of value to customers in digital markets, which we have named the *marketspace*. This is a primarily digital environment that – through the assembly and management of a cohesive set of services across an entire area of customer concern (for example childcare, sport, learning, fashion and so on) – solves the major value problems facing customers and businesses in the current situation.

We proceed to examine – at a high level again – the key drivers and enablers that will, we believe, support the evolution of marketspace-type offerings, focusing in particular upon technical issues.

Moving to the last of our three halves, Chapters 9 and 10 – 'Roles and Benefits in Marketspaces' and 'Rules and Relationships in Marketspaces' – may be best dipped into as your current particular needs dictate. Departing slightly from the more narrative-based argument that features in the rest of the book, they are designed to assist businesses from a range of industry sectors to identify and consider their ideal stances, should they wish to engage with the marketspace paradigm.

We conclude the book by examining – using our final key tool, the 'Value Cube' – where the various degrees of customer and business value will lie in future digital markets. Our key arguments are then recapped, to bring the book to what we hope is a gentle landing after an occasionally challenging flight!

The rules of the game

We use several little techniques that we hope will make *Promiscuous Customers* an easy and satisfying read.

'Key point' (self-explanatory of course) indicates where we feel an especially important statement is made. 'Hard hat area' – rarely used in fact – tells you that what follows may be a little dense for certain readers and, while the contents are important, they can be flipped through at a headline level without seriously compromising the overall read. 'He said … she said …' signals a quote from or reference to a relevant comment from another source, while 'Back in the real world' introduces brief case studies that illustrate the argument with reference to the present day.

Overall, you'll notice that the reading experience does by necessity become slightly more demanding as the book progresses. Two reasons for this:

First of all we are, as the book moves forward, engaging with more substantial issues of technical and business strategy … to shy away from these would be to betray both your needs and ours. A major misconception that drove the dot-com fiasco was that somehow this is all terribly easy. Far from it: trade in digital markets is more complex, more expensive and more risky than any seen before.

Secondly, while the earlier part of the book deconstructs and criticises what will tend to be familiar concepts, we then proceed to introduce quite new thinking that – while building, we hope, on a solid foundation of value-based thinking – nevertheless features its own frameworks and vocabulary that will demand greater effort from you.

But we do ask that you stick with it … it's worth it!

NOTES

1   By this we mean commercial environments that are accessed through one or more digital channels (the Internet, the World Wide Web, mobile, interactive TV etc.).

2   ActivMedia, quoted by Nua (www.nua.ie).

3   Forrester Research, quoted by Nua (www.nua.ie).

4   A.T. Kearney, 'Satisfying the Experienced On-line Shopper', report, 2000.

5   Elmwood, 'Does it click?', report, 2001.

6   The Blade Partnership, a consortium of WPP companies including The Henley Centre, 2001.

7   GartnerGroup (1999).

8   See Chapter 4, 'Modes, Purposes and Tasks'.

CHAPTER 1

The Cold Heart of the Promiscuous Customer

'Now here, you see, it takes all the running you can do to keep in the same place. If you want to get somewhere else, you must run at least twice as fast as that!'

IN THIS CHAPTER WE LOOK AT

- the new service challenges posed by digital markets;
- the expectations of the on-line customer;
- the problem of loyalty;
- the strategic red herring of CRM; and
- the emergence of meaning and trust as fundamental service and value drivers in digital markets.

THE MIRAGE OF LOYALTY

Infinite choice, infinite access, infinite expectation

Today's customers in digital markets are, like spoilt children, both fortified and frustrated by an impression of almost infinite choice. When there's always another supplier at my fingertips, always a better deal around the corner, and I have access to these through a plethora of channels and devices, is it any surprise that I feel no need to bond with a particular supplier?

Each new service standard that's set simply raises the bar; added value rapidly degrades into perceived commodity.

The lack of human contact, traditionally a reliable means to encourage bonding and build brand loyalty, further sharply reduces the range of opportunity for personal service and shared problem-solving.

'20 SECONDS TO COMPLY ...'

The golden years of terrible service

Put yourself in the shoes of yesterday's customer for a couple of minutes. Say you drove past a billboard promoting a special offer where a freephone number was featured for you to order a brochure – perhaps this was promoting a financial services company. You jotted down or remembered the number and sometime later you rang up to order your free information pack. You sat on hold for maybe five minutes, listening to elevator music, or perhaps a snippet of baroque that was just intrusive enough to prevent you from thinking about anything else while you waited – or should we say while you *wasted* your time, which somehow didn't seem quite so valuable back then.

Eventually a call-centre staff member picked up your call. They could be pretty brusque with you, because they were clearly busy, otherwise why would you have waited for so long? So you

INTRODUCING OUR PLAYERS...

Introducing Christopher Marlowe and Janet Weiss. These two individuals (who don't know each other, by the way; they live on different continents) will be protagonists in some of the case studies and examples we'll be using in the rest of the book.

Janet Weiss is a teacher, aged 37, married to Brad, with a son of 8 named Rocky. They live in Amarillo, Texas. Janet teaches science in a large public school in the city, usually children with an age range of 10–13. Janet's personal interests include country music, cookery and Native American art.

Currently Janet is using the World Wide Web to:

- Source and purchase teaching aids of various kinds, including books, scientific kit, some (usually non-critical) research materials.
- Keep track of the relevant aspects of her curriculum, supported mainly by federally- and locally-funded and maintained sites dedicated to the teaching community.
- Participate in a small range of on-line discussion groups, covering both professional and personal concerns. She takes a particular interest in the management of violent behaviour in the classroom. Her son Rocky suffers from a serious food allergy, and she actively supports a national on-line anaphylaxis resource discussion group.
- She has also signed onto a comparable range of email newsletters.

Janet uses a laptop at home, with a 56k dial-up line; at school, the local area network provides high-speed access to the Internet; she is a regular if infrequent mobile phone user.

Christopher Marlowe is a freelance industrial designer, aged 41, who lives in South London. He is divorced, with an active role

17

in the parenting of his son of 13, William. Already an established and experienced user of technology in his working life, Christopher was an early convert to the Internet, and it features heavily in his day-to-day life. His personal interests include yoga, classical music and junk crime novels.

Christopher uses the World Wide Web to:

- Collaborate, on a more or less daily basis, with colleagues and clients on project work, using whiteboard and other virtual conferencing tools with comfort.
- Shop for books and music, using a combination of well-known and more esoteric outlets.
- Participate – admittedly with little regularity or enthusiasm – in a very small number of discussion groups relating to his profession. In contrast, his son William has a surprising – and rare at his age – passion for poetry, and they both belong to a small online community of enthusiasts.
- Like Janet, Christopher receives a range of email newsletters (many of which he wishes he'd never signed up for, but can't find the time to unsubscribe ...)

Christopher has a fairly new and powerful laptop for both work and personal use and as a freelancer is a very frequent mobile phone user, often sending and receiving email through his state-of-

sympathised with them, and they took down your details. You politely said goodbye.

A week later nothing had come. Still feeling basically OK about this company, you rang back. It turned out that your previous service contact had taken down your address wrongly, and your new friend in the call centre promised that the package would go out tonight to the correct address.

Eventually the package arrived. And – if indeed they'd sent you the right materials – despite your fairly negative experience of the company's service thus far, you probably remained at least receptive to their offer. In other words, *no critical damage to perceived value or trust was done* by this quite extensive catalogue of service errors, spread over a period of perhaps two weeks. And you may indeed have become a customer.

The instant damage of poor customer experience

Fast forward to today. The same financial services company brings to your attention a similar offering, with a link to a dedicated mini-site for you to visit. But likely due to no fault of the company – maybe your service provider's having a bad day – there's a problem with speed of download. You feel the bile rising within say 20 seconds ... eventually an over-large graphics file begins its slow appearance on your screen.[1]

One touch on the back button, and you're gone. And you'll never be a customer of that firm, and you may say a few disparaging things about them and their offer to friends, just for good measure.

Because you know how good service can be online, because you've experienced it before, you know that someone's just wasted your time, which has recently become – now that you're a spoiled 'promiscuous customer' – as valuable as gold dust. Just like in the film,[2] that company had '20 seconds to comply ... ' to your needs, in your timeframe. It failed, and got blown away forever.

Somehow, in digital markets, the expectations of our most valuable customers are almost absurdly heightened and accelerated. And they're inclined to shoot first – assassinating the brand with remarkable callousness – and not bothering to ask any questions at all ...

How then are businesses to address what seems to be a progressive and insoluble problem? How are customers to be attracted and retained?

THE RED HERRING OF CUSTOMER RELATIONSHIP MANAGEMENT

If customer loyalty is acknowledged as one of the biggest challenges facing business today, it's so easy to respond by making the critical mistake of placing the cart of Customer Relationship Management (CRM) in front of the horses of trust and value.

The customer's cold heart

There's been a traditional sentimentality – a sort of fond avuncular soppiness – in marketing's approach to and treatment of customers, which has perhaps peaked recently in the rush of enthusiasm for CRM.

But, as it's turning out, a lot of customers don't seem terribly impressed, and few loyalty programs seem to deliver the value they promised. It seems that customers aren't as keen as businesses on this notion of 'managed loyalty', and more often than not fail to see the value to them of this relationship.

There's equally a big question mark over the issue of whether these initiatives create any real value for the business. And, at the time of writing, at least one major technology player has pulled in its horns sharply on the subject …

KEY POINT

We must be clear on this point. CRM is at its best only a system that enables more powerful, consistent, and economical capture and leveraging of the customer value and trust that have already been established in the various contacts that make up the history of the relationship so far. Without these, a CRM program is simply empty of relevance to the customer, and can indeed turn on its owners – to cannibalise both loyalty and reputation – by throwing into relief the very problems they seek to fix.

HE SAID ... SHE SAID...

'Ironically, the very things that marketeers are doing to build relationships with customers are often the things that are destroying
those relationships.'

'Preventing the Premature Death of Relationship Marketing', *Harvard Business Review*, January 1998.

'As buyers' initial curiosity with the Web wanes and subsidies end,
companies offering products and services on-line will be forced
to demonstrate that they provide real benefits. Already, customers
appear to be losing interest in services like Priceline's reverse auctions, because the savings they provide are often outweighed by
the hassles involved. As customers become more familiar with the
technology, their loyalty to their initial suppliers will also decline;
they will realise that the cost of switching is low.'

'Strategy and the Internet', *Harvard Business Review*, March
2001.

there's been talk of a new 'C-MR', or Customer-Managed Relationships.

Whether or not you buy – and we have our own doubts on
this – that promiscuous customers can actually be bothered (why
should they?) to take on an active role in a relationship for which
they've rarely demonstrated even a passive interest in the past,
there's a growing perception among even the most vocal and
committed proponents of managed loyalty that the customer is in
charge.

So, while there's no doubt that many of the principles of 1:1
are sound (to the point perhaps of being tautological) the assumption that the best way to the customer's cold heart is by relationship-building is by no means a sound one and no more so than in
digital markets.

A SUPERMARKET EPIPHANY, OR LOYALTY AS COMMODITY

A leading British supermarket group made a big splash with its loyalty card scheme in the mid-nineties. Christopher signed up for it, as did millions of other shoppers. Within two years of the program's launch the company had taken leadership in its market.

It was easy to assume that the chain had seized this lead in the market due to this shrewd stealing of a CRM march. But soon enough the major competitors' own faltering efforts got on their feet, and things got busier in the supermarket loyalty card area. As the competitors' programs took root, consumers like Christopher got smart, unsurprisingly rather liking the idea of getting paid for their custom wherever they shopped, however often they came back and however much they spent.

It soon became clear that the promise of personalisation was being delivered to the consumer in the most clumsy fashion … Far from analysing purchasing patterns and then coming back with a more refined offer, the only clear evidence of activity was a remarkable increase in mailings from various 'partners' of the chain. This was not going to build anything other than the most mercenary and cynical loyalty.

Owning information about an individual and their purchasing behaviour is not synonymous with having any sort of relationship with that individual. It is at the point of contact where the customer is actively seeking value from the business that the most important opportunities – and indeed risks – for relationship building appear.

KEY POINT

The customer relationship exists – and is therefore built or destroyed, grown or eroded – at the interface. Not in the database.

WHAT REALLY MATTERS TO CUSTOMERS IN DIGITAL MARKETS

Time for us to introduce two fundamental concepts to our discussion, those of *meaning* and *trust*.

Meaning in digital markets

If products and services meet the customer need in the off-line economy, in digital markets – where information is the basic currency – it is, we contend, *meaning* that determines how a customer relates (especially with any sort of loyalty) to a business. It is meaning that conveys to the mind of the customer the potential value represented by competitive offerings.

Indeed, it is in so many instances a thirst for meaning that underlies the strategic disarray in the e-commerce environment at the turn of the century. As we'll see below mere information – as the unmapped sea in which our islands of patchy value sit in isolation – does nothing better than erode value.

Meaning, as we're using the term here, is about *making sense of things*. Note that information (or worse even, data) does not intrinsically aid us in making sense of the world. A shared sense of meaning is equally essential to effective communication and useful community. If you can't make sense, you can't be informed, make decisions, communicate or, of course, transact.

A question of trust

Trust is, in any environment – personal or business, on- or off-line – developed by affirming and building upon an initial commitment (which is an 'act of faith') through the effective ongoing management of various types of real and perceived risk.

As the initial 'act of faith' leads into a series of hopefully positive encounters, it is alchemised into real trust, with this process taking the form of a trail of right answers to the sometimes simple, sometimes complex, but invariably important questions posed by the customer.

THE SLOPING PLAYING FIELD, THE MOVING GOALPOSTS

Promiscuous customers in digital markets remain unimpressed by sentimental attempts at building loyalty in the absence of authentic meaning and trust. They respond quickly, decisively and negatively to interruptive communications, and any unreasonable delays in service delivery are punished by immediate erosion of brand loyalty. As we've seen above, these little 'betrayals' attack both meaning and trust, fundamentally undermining any attempt to deliver value, and of course placing anything resembling loyalty way out of reach.

Only when these complex challenges are fully met by businesses, will on-line relationship-building initiatives finally find any sort of fertile ground.

Every single encounter – no matter how fleeting or apparently unimportant – with brands in digital markets provides a real-time opportunity to either incrementally build or fatally wound this fragile bond with promiscuous customers. We need to accept that the effort and cost involved in satisfying their fickle and ever more demanding needs may, in more than a few cases, simply not be worthwhile for the business.

MEANING AND TRUST IN ACTION

For a closer look at just how central meaning and trust are to the performance of digital markets, and also in order to introduce several key components of both today's and tomorrow's environments, let's examine some brief examples.

Information without context and credibility

Janet's using the Web to hunt for information – in this case, some background material for a class chemistry project she's creating for the next term. There is of course an infinity of free information on the Web, but it's all over the place. Using the usual search engines and directories, she comes up with a long list of possible Web pages to explore. Some look very promising yet turn out to be junk. Some of the most humble looking results, on the other hand, emerge as the most credible, and using the bookmarking facility in her browser she creates a shortlist of say 15 sites for closer examination.

At the end of this long process, Janet may emerge triumphant with two or three reasonable results. But – and this is in no sense an attack on the many excellent search engines that do sterling service at the time of writing – neither meaning nor trust are well-served. Janet's task requires that she must first sort through a plethora of largely irrelevant – often laughable – material to create her shortlist, which remains largely devoid of trustworthiness.

So, despite 'all that information out there', in this instance Janet has still needed to work hard and long to create her own meaning. At the end of that process, she also needs to take the risk of making her own judgement call about the credibility of the material she selects as being relevant to her needs. So the environment brings her no trust either.

This is hardly customer heaven, is it? Lacking are a meaningful context and credible (in this case, expert) endorsement and certification of information that could possibly put pupils at risk in the laboratory. So, Janet has to first work hard (the very volume of information on-line typically creates extra work – erodes value in other words – for customers in today's digital markets). Then she must take the risk of assigning her own (admittedly informed but not necessarily expert) approval to whatever material she selects for use on the project. Information, in the absence of services that provide meaning and trust, creates extra work and risk for customers.

Trust services – prevention, cure or cynical sticking plaster?
Christopher's search for an obscure jazz title has brought him – surfing the Web one lunchtime (surely not on client time!) – to a new on-line shop that claims to specialise in just what he's looking for … but the business appears to be based in Belgium, and Chris has never heard of it or bought from it until now.

The homepage of City Slicker Sounds does carry the logos of more than one known trust brand, but two questions need answering – that is, if Christopher feels any sense of doubt or hesitation before committing to a purchase: first of all, what do these marks of trust actually mean, in terms of a commitment to the customer? Do they mean that whatever happens here, the customer's protected? Or is it in fact only the business that's protected from the fraudulent customer? What sort of 'protection' are we talking about? Is it just that this business has paid some money to a trust brand to sign up to a code of practice? How many customers understand what trust brands mean?

Coming back to Christopher's current encounter, his only comment (as a designer) might be that the all-important trust marks feature prominently on the homepage, but promptly disappear for the rest of his encounter with City Slicker, including the point at which he decides to purchase the disc, arranges fulfilment and confirms payment. Are these marks really about certification, or simply cynical marketing tools?

So trust services suffer from a lack of meaning, and their very trustworthiness – certainly on closer inspection by the customer – is typically far from clearly conveyed.

TO SUMMARISE

- Service in digital markets is a far more demanding imperative than business has experienced before, while the benchmark of adequacy is constantly raised, and customer loyalty remains independent of satisfactory performance.
- Thus we describe our customer in digital markets as promiscuous – highly demanding, unsentimental, and generally unwilling to assign loyalty.
- Customer Relationship Management is, while being an important support activity, both a tautology and a strategic red herring. While optimising the collection and application of customer data is simple common sense for many businesses, in the absence of meaning, trust and subsequently value and commitment, CRM programs in fact attack loyalty.

NOTES

1   Note of course that lengthy downloads *per se* are not detrimental. It's when the customer's time is wasted with low value and/or inadequate relevance, that the damage is done.

2   That film was, of course, *Robocop*. (Dating ourselves here, sadly …)

CHAPTER 2

The Paradox of
the Invisible Brand

'... I wish you wouldn't keep appearing and vanishing so suddenly: you make one quite giddy!'

'All right', said the Cat; and this time it vanished quite slowly, beginning with the end of the tail, and ending with the grin which remained some time after the rest of it had gone.

IN THIS CHAPTER WE LOOK AT

- the fundamental new brand issues that arise in digital markets;
- the unprecedented immediacy and reality of the customer's encounter with this *invisible brand*;
- some past blind alleys deriving from serious misunderstandings regarding the invisible brand; and
- the new challenges that arise for brand and design management.

THE 'THIRD WAVE' OF THE BRAND ENCOUNTER

Things are happening to brands again ...

Let's look at a very simplified history to set some context for our look at how brands are starting to behave in digital markets.

Brands began life as a means of *distinguishing and attaching trust* to a product. In this 'First Wave', the brand says to the customer: 'We're OK, and you're OK with us.' With good luck and management, trust becomes preference and preference evolves into loyalty. The First Wave relationship is a functional one, with relatively prosaic aspects of the product like consistency, predictability and safety to the fore.

Eventually, some brands began to detach from specific products, and became *attached to dream lifestyles*. The branded product or service in this Second Wave is in a way the customer's 'ticket to the dream'. This brand says: 'We're over here! Why not join us?' This brand also says 'We're OK with you ... as long as you have the right ticket.'

So in the Second Wave, product function moves to the back seat and the aspirations of the customer, peer influence and, in some instances, social position, come into play. It's also been argued that this Second Wave brand goes some way towards filling the hole left by – at least in Western consumer society – the decline of organised religion and family values.

What does need to be noted for our current purpose is how – compared with the typically warm but hardly passionate tone of the First Wave – the Second Wave brand, by necessity, packs a hefty emotional charge. Rightly or wrongly, my bond with the dream lifestyle brands – sneakers or German cars or coffee bars – whose products I invest in (and that investment typically takes the form of far more than just money or time, by the way) is powerful, emotive and very complex.

HE SAID ... SHE SAID ...

'What exactly is a brand? It is a word that is so over-used that we rarely stop to consider what it actually means. The brand concept is complex, and different people define brands in different ways. Some focus on the brand as trademark, such as David Aaker from the University of California, Berkeley, for whom it is: "A distinguishing name and/or symbol (such as a logo, trademark or package design) intended to identify the goods or services of either one seller or a group of sellers, and to differentiate those goods or services from those of competitors." Others, such as Jean-Noel Kapferer at the HEC School of Management in Paris, fix on what it means to the consumer: "A brand is not a product. It is the product's essence, its meaning, and its direction, and it defines its identity in time and space." This is a view to a large extent supported by Stephen King from the J. Walter Thompson advertising agency: "A product is something made in a factory; a brand is something bought by a customer. A product can be copied by a competitor; a brand is unique. A product can be quickly outdated; a brand is timeless."

'But a full definition of the brand surely encompasses both perspectives. It is a combination of a set of trademarks (brand name, logo, etc.) as well as consumers' perceptions and expectations of products and services branded with these trademarks.'

Brand.new, ed. Jane Pavitt, V & A Publications, 2000

WHAT DO YOU DO WHEN THE MEDIUM IS THE PRODUCT?

But in digital markets, the customer's 'Third Wave' encounter with the brand is a very different one. If previous manifestations of brand have been attached to products, and subsequently to dream lifestyles, *the digital brand is embedded in the user's immersive experience*. Logo or no logo, this Third Wave brand is invisible.

THE MEDIUM AS (NO LONGER THE MESSAGE ...) THE PRODUCT

Janet receives, via a commercial childcare site, a monthly update – with occasional extra bulletins – on food allergy issues. This is of particular interest to Janet and Brad since, as we mentioned previously, their son Rocky has a serious food allergy that can lead to possibly fatal anaphylactic shock. In other words, this is a matter of life and death.

Not that they rely solely on an email service to manage this intimidating responsibility in their lives – far from it – but the service is a valuable and personalised one. The association of the brand owner, say 'KidZone.com', with this service is highly positive, but any excessive branding, any over-proprietary handling of the communication, severely compromises the perceived quality and credibility of the service. Yes, it's trust and meaning again.

Christopher's looking with William for a book by a respected New Zealand poet, Kelvin Allen, whose new work has taken their fancy. At the time of writing, Amazon will typically be their first port of call, although there do exist plenty of smaller, niche on-line retailers who specialise in poetry.

Note that their experience, despite the 2D nature of the experience of a PC monitor, is very much an 'immersive' one, in the sense that they're encountering – with the exception of course of the product itself which will arrive later – every aspect of the Amazon service. In this sense their experience is far more akin to that of a service brand than a product brand: at every turn their encounter modifies their impressions of and feelings about the brand of Amazon. They're touching sales, service, inventory, retail environment, advice, community (the other poetry fiends have lots to say about Kelvin Allen's work), fulfilment, payment, relationship management and so on.

See how different this encounter is from an equivalent series of brand contacts in off-line environments?

The medium that was once the message, once taken into digital markets is now the product … even the business itself.

'In what sense should one consider a screen desktop less real than any other?… I feel no sense of unreality in my relationship to any of these objects … In the culture of simulation, if it works for you, it has all the reality it needs.'

Sherry Turkle in *Life on the Screen*[1]

KEY POINT

Let's be very clear here. Getting behind that feeble word 'virtual', we see that the customer encounter with the brand on-line is actually closer, more direct and more real than any previously.

From the same important work, here's a nervous chat-room user describing her feelings about a first face-to-face meeting with an on-line friend:

'I didn't exactly lie to him about anything specific, but I feel very different on-line. I am a lot more outgoing, less inhibited. I would say that I feel more like myself. But that's a contradiction. I feel like more who I wish I was. I'm just hoping that face-to-face I can find a way to spend some time being the on-line me.'

Does the word 'virtual' really mean anything any more? Can we continue to deny the startling immediacy of the digital encounter with the Invisible Brand?

A BRIEF ASIDE ON THE NATURE OF REALITY

The 17th-century English philosopher Bishop Berkeley argued (and indeed he has yet to be effectively challenged) that our apparently direct, real-time encounter with the world is in fact impossible to prove. Since we can only encounter 'the world' through our senses, and since those senses are both infinitely unreliable and individual to each us, how can we prove the existence of anything outside the isolated dream of our own perceptions? And how can we claim in any sense to share that reality with each other?

We raise this to underpin our point. Despite their location in physical existence, in many ways the common manifestations of the First and Second Wave brands, as found in packaging, in point-of-sale material, in the hands of the perfect housewife on the TV etc., are encountered by the customer in a manner that is quite removed from 'reality'.

Compare this corner-of-the-eye, twilight meeting with the analogue brand, with the immediate, real time, cause-and-effect impact of the digital experience.

If, as we saw above, life on the screen is no less real to the user than the encounter with physical reality, for how much longer can we hold onto the false notion that the digital encounter with the brand is any less real, any less important and impactful, than the 'analogue' one?

We argue that, to the contrary, it is more so, not less.

KEY POINT

The paradox of the Invisible Brand

In digital markets therefore, the customer's encounter with the brand occurs in the most sterile and inhuman of environments, and typically lacks any meaningful emotional charge.

Yet this is, at the same time, the most real encounter that any customer has yet had with any brand and with any business: the environment for the encounter, the communications, the service, the transactions, the support … they all combine to surround the customer both immersively and intimately.

INTRODUCING PURPOSES AND TASKS

This meeting with the brand (and smaller, low-bandwidth touchpoints are no exception here: this is not immersion in the sense of VR – that most real but least meaningful of virtual experiences) is up-close and personal. It is in fact driven by the purpose that has brought the customer to the space, and the necessary tasks that derive from that purpose.

AND BACK IN THE REAL WORLD...

Japan's Men Date Hot, Sexy Bots

by Michelle Delio

2:00 a.m. Nov. 28, 2000 PST

At least 30,000 Japanese men are happily practising their romantic skills by attempting to virtually woo and win a girlfriend via a mobile phone matchmaking service.

Subscribers to the 'Love By Mail' service get to choose their girlfriend from a lineup of women that includes a bartender, a flight attendant, an office worker and a teacher. Once they've made a selection, they can begin to date the woman via e-mail.

But Love By Mail participants don't simply exchange giggly e-mails that rapidly escalate to more graphic love letters.

The men must carefully gauge their romantic moves. Those who promise too much or don't move fast enough won't impress their woman, and will get bitter e-mails in response. Likewise, those who attempt to talk about sports or offer excuses about needing to work too often will also get the cold shoulder from their new love.

Successful seducers are rewarded by increasingly romantic e-mails from their sweetheart, in which she gradually reveals her 'most intimate secrets'.

But there is one catch – the women the men are corresponding with are nothing more than pre-programmed computer scripts.

That doesn't seem to bother Love By Mail's intrepid subscribers.

http://www.wired.com/news/print/0,1294,40369,00.html

SO ... WHAT DOES THE THIRD WAVE BRAND HAVE TO SAY?

This is why, while the customer may have some fleeting posses-sion of the First or Second Wave brand, in digital markets he or she owns the freehold! The promiscuous customer owns her own private day-to-day electronic experiences of your business, and the sum of these – up to and including today's – is what the brand rep-resents to her.

So, the Third Wave brand could be said to be the promiscu-ous customer's name for the sum of her encounters with your business in digital markets to date. This is an Invisible Brand.

Does this Invisible Brand have anything at all to say? Of course. But the only vocabulary that the promiscuous customer wants to hear – at least in the on-line environment – is the lan-guage of meaning, trust and value. This brand has a lot to say. But get this: it speaks only when it's spoken to.

THE EMPEROR'S INVISIBLE CLOTHES

Companies! No trespassing!

We talked just now about the emotional charge that hard-hitting, dream lifestyle, aspirational Second Wave brands typically seek to create. And in the early days of on-line corporate communications, the mistake of mixing up this Second Wave with the cold, demanding Third Wave environment was so common it was almost universal.

There was talk of 'compelling content', of irresistibly 'sticky' Web sites, of magnetic 'communities of interest', of 'delighting the on-line customer' and so on.

And let's be clear – these environments did and still do exist, but sadly they're 'true', (i.e., private, user-driven) communities of interest, where the intrusions of self-interested, profit-driven cor-porations are considered a hostile affront to the *raison d'être* of the entire space.

I OWN MY BANK ...

We mentioned earlier that the model of a service brand tends to bear the most fruit in the quest to understand how customers connect with the Invisible Brand in digital markets. Let's look at Christopher's recent contact cycle[2] with his bank, which has recently relaunched its on-line service as an Internet-based facility.

He'd been very happy with the PC-based service the bank had provided previously, and had taken considerable time to install, learn and regularly use the product, YourBucks 1.0. His overall experience with the bank, his receptiveness to the inevitable regular cross-selling attempts, and whatever meagre loyalty he felt towards the bank's brand, were all reasonably robust.

A representative of the bank phoned him one evening and asked how happy he had been with YourBucks. He replied, yes, fine. Would he be willing to change over to their new Web-based service, WebWonga.com, launching in three months? Since he'd invested quite a bit of time in YourBucks, he said, well, probably not. At which point the representative sprung the cunning trap: he had no choice, because a further three months after the launch of WebWonga, YourBucks was to be discontinued.

A strange approach to a fairly valuable customer that left Christopher feeling angry and compromised. From a point of some comfort, the bank's brand had rapidly gone into the doghouse. He told a lot of friends about this nasty trick the bank had played (and by the way, this is based on a real experience in the UK), but eventually calmed down and signed up for the first iteration of WebWonga.

The quality of the experience was initially well below that of YourBucks, which had felt very secure and predictable. In contrast, WebWonga felt far too 'webby': there seemed to be no end to the variety of problems he encountered in the early months, some of course not originating with the bank, but all contributing towards a general drop in trust in the brand.

To make matters a little worse, there was the steady stream of mailings from the bank asking him to sign up now for a year's free use of WebWonga. Christopher felt that he shouldn't be paying for the service at all, since the bank was clearly saving many millions with WebWonga, and the quality was still not great.

What's happening here? Christopher's making contact with the brand of his bank in various ways over time. Some encounters have been good, some not so good. At each point in the contact cycle, his own 'personal version' of the bank's brand rises and falls, ebbs and flows, strengthens and weakens, dependent entirely upon the quality – largely the meaning and trust, in fact – of his most recent experience.

In digital markets, this brand can no longer be substantially massaged upwards. When the medium is the product, we stand or fall almost solely by the quality – or lack of it – in these mundane encounters. And that quality is almost entirely defined in terms of the support – or lack thereof – that is provided for customer purposes and tasks.

Bludgeoned by compelling, sticky content

Anyway, we rushed in on this buzz of on-line opportunity ... and tried either to import the emotional charge of the Second Wave brand on-line in a wholesale fashion, or to invent entirely new sorts of powerful screen-based experience. The idea seemed to be to lock in the newly on-line customer (who perhaps at that time was a little less jaded and intolerant of such screen candy) with a hypnotic display of emotionally-charged, vaguely brand-linked content and function.

Of course, in gaming sites and other pure entertainment-based environments, a whole other set of rules applies, and the user mode is utterly different – playful, tolerant of (as long as it's fun) interruption, and far less obsessively purpose-driven and task-focused.)

The sinking of the bloated Web site

Was this deep misplacement of value caused in part by the fact that so many early new media professionals came in from content – from entertainment or publishing? Or was this caused by the fact that many of these initiatives were creatively driven – if not always implemented – by the big advertising networks? Or is this just a particularly expensive example of the gap between 'multimedia' and e-business?

We had an auto manufacturing site that went up to close to 40,000 pages, we had another auto manufacturer taking the 'community of interest' idea so drastically far that they were practically advising customers on how to part their hair and which jeans to buy … We even had a leading bank with drug references on its homepage. We were way off-strategy, off-brand, off-voice, off-mode … we were off the wall.

And soon enough, we had to pull our horns in and refocus on what communicating and doing business in digital markets really meant. The damage that was done to the marketing budget (where almost all this money came from, after all), with paltry or typically negative returns, woke us up.

Now, we're thrown back again on the delivery of value as being what customers want, before and over and above any other contact that we may wish to have with them.

THE ONLY WAY IS DOWN?

Let's ask this question boldly, and then step back and consider its consequences.

In the dry, sterile environment that is the context for the customer's digital encounter with a business and its brands, just how can 'off-task' or 'off-mode' communications from the business add any meaningful value for the promiscuous customer?

The bulk of the value that the customer extracts in digital markets is divorced from any sentimental considerations and derived from the uncluttered, rapid provision of relevant service. How then can a branded environment ever provide more than an adequate, 'message-neutral' space within which the customer and the value he or she seeks can do their dance?

We believe that marketing messages and other interruptive, off-mode activity must be walled off from the customer's focused, task-driven attention. They will need to be catered for with a separate set of customer permissions and behavioural protocols, and in many cases using different touchpoints. The only alternative we can see is that our promiscuous customers will tire of this increasingly irrelevant harassment and desert the offending business for less intrusive services.

SO WHAT DO THESE CHALLENGES MEAN FOR BRAND MANAGEMENT?

'Bringing up' the Invisible Brand

Out of sight, out of mind, out of control
In digital markets, brands also spend much of their existence outside the owner's authority, within affiliates' sites, search engines, directories and channel guides. Once peer distribution through e-mail, file sharing, SMS, discussion groups or hate sites enters the picture, the owner loses almost all control. So brands require resilient features that, as far as possible, let their principal characteristics survive in out-of-control environments.

Customers carry their own perception of the brand around with them. This perception can be enhanced by appropriate brand behaviour and interactions and is instantly damaged by any poor

HANDS OFF THE CUSTOMER PLEASE

Janet's heard through word of mouth about a new test for food allergies that will indicate with a high degree of reliability whether sufferers could benefit from an important new treatment. This is not only directly relevant to her son Rocky's condition, but is also of course a subject of major concern to the whole family.

Knowing that Janet is – for obvious reasons – a likely customer for this new service, do we find ways to intrude into her experience as she searches around the Web, using her known resources, search engines, and perhaps discussion groups to find out more about the new test? Of course not. It's worth noting that, where the customer's purpose in digital markets is one of high personal concern, the intrusions of – quite conceivably appropriate – extra messages are about as welcome (and ultimately as beneficial to the business) as a cheerleader at a funeral.

experience. And the effect is not isolated: just as positive experience can lead to peer recommendation, so bad experience can rapidly lead to negative messaging and active denigration.

So brand development may now be about 'bringing up' the brand – equipping it for life in the full spectrum of environments it will encounter, and minimising its potential for provoking antagonism.

The brand as roaming ambassador

Like a tough, experienced and sleek diplomat, tomorrow's Invisible Brand glides through the infinitely complex, infinitely changeable, frequently hostile worlds in which it now lives.

The limitless range of challenges it will face makes any consistency of appearance nothing less than a hazard – this brand is a chameleon. Yet its tone of voice must slice instantly and recognisably through cultural and linguistic barriers – as well as the endless and rising cacophony of its competitors.

Wherever it finds itself, the Invisible Brand must negotiate new value for its masters by recognising – with lightning speed – the natures, needs and wants of the customers and prospects it meets, and delivering value through meeting mode with meaning, trust, and value.

AND HOW ABOUT DESIGN MANAGEMENT?

Through the looking glass

At the time of writing, one need only spend a few months as a regular Amazon customer[3] or AvantGo user to know without question that the hand of great design is at work in the creation of today's most trusted on-line environments.

Design remains the only discipline that can take ownership of the creation of the environments where user needs and business services meet with optimum relevance and value for both sides.

Can design accept that, alongside its more dramatic creative breakthroughs, it also has a humbler yet absolutely central role to play in managing those tiny, critical encounters with invisible brands that, if we're lucky, support some kind of trust and foster some kind of loyalty?

TO SUMMARISE

- A completely new paradigm for the analysis and management of brands is required for digital markets (irrespective of a brand's off-line heritage).
- When customers encounter brands in this cold environment, the meeting is paradoxically both highly direct and impactfuland devoid of any substantial emotional component.

- The nature of the encounter wrests ownership of the Invisible Brand away from the owner and assigns it to the customer, whose most prosaic and elementary experiences of service and relevance are the primary drives of perceived value.
- Historically, traditional marketing's failure to grasp the profound shift in brand management and communication issues has caused a value-eroding over-focus on content and stickiness, where the customer's real expectations of service and value have been studiously ignored in the pursuit of old-style share of time and mind share.
- Both design and brand management urgently need to reconsider their roles and priorities in their approach to the Invisible Brand: in particular a concentration upon process is demanded. At the same time, they need to accept that brands in digital markets are intrinsically out of control, and that therefore a new 'hands-off' philosophy of brand management is in order.

NOTES

1   Sherry Turkle, *Life on the Screen*, New York, Simon and Schuster 1997.

2   By 'contact cycle' we mean the series of significant events that make up the history of a customer's relationship with a brand.

3   Note, by the way, that no less than 70% of Amazon's total IT budget is spent on supply chain and other service infrastructure, only 30% on their world-class Web site.

CHAPTER 3

What's Wrong with the Internet?

'The rule is, jam tomorrow and jam yesterday, but never jam today.'

IN THIS CHAPTER WE LOOK AT

- techniques for describing business models in today's 'Commoditised Internet';
- the enormous challenges facing most businesses in that environment, in particular the stripping of value, and the resulting elusiveness of sustainable business and revenue models; and
- the corresponding frustrations facing customers, including the fragmentation of their typical experience, the alienation of information from customer task, the negative effect of multiple devices, and the overall paucity of value.

A MUCH TOUGHER GAME ALL ROUND

We've looked already at the customer experience in digital markets at the turn of the century, and at some of the things that are taking brands and brand owners by surprise. Let's turn now to businesses themselves, and the problems they face, in what we call the Commoditised Internet.

At the time of writing, summer 2001, any business trading profitably and with shareholder confidence in digital markets is very big news. Even the darlings of the stock markets – notably the hitherto robust Yahoo! and even core technology suppliers like Cisco – are suffering. Allowing for the backlash to the tulip fever that peaked in early 2000 before the rapid drop in dot-com share prices, clearly the way forward to value for digital business is far from clear.

The pulling in of horns among previously free-spending and confident media and content owners such as Disney and News Corporation signals that maybe content isn't king[1] after all. There's a corresponding contraction on the supply side, as the pure digital agencies tighten their belts and traditional marketing firms and advertising networks (correctly) question their future roles. The happy memory of the absurd dot-com spend-fest recedes and the interruptive communications model gets leakier all the time.

So what has crushed that buoyant optimism? What's wrong, if you like, with the Internet?

SEARCHING FOR VALUE

How we analyse digital markets

Let's start by distinguishing the main types of Internet business from each other. We use a simple approach to differentiate 'business models' in digital markets. Perhaps surprisingly, the majority of the much-discussed new business models can be characterised as one or other combination of a few relatively simple features. The model under scrutiny is mapped in three dimensions across the following axes.

The primary offer – what's in it for the customer?

The first question we ask, unsurprisingly, is 'what is the service offering to its customers?' In other words the *business proposition*. For the purpose of analysis we look at the nature of the product in terms both of its form, tangible or intangible, and its properties, product or service. From this we derive a spectrum of types ranging from the provision of information and navigation services only (e.g., news, search engines), through entertainment and intangible products (e.g., software and financial services) to tangible products, or hard goods (e.g., books, PCs and so on).

This axis is summarised in Fig. 3.1. The diagram also illustrates another simple, but significant, truth about the implied customer relationship: products to the left are essentially ephemeral services like news and entertainment whose consumption is simultaneous with their use, those to the right imply a longer-term contact with both product and, potentially, supplier.

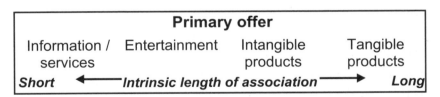

Fig. 3.1 Categorising the spectrum of products provided by a digital service.

The business driver – the core business model

The second axis examines the *key success factor*, what the operator must achieve if it is to generate revenue from the enterprise. For example, if the service is to be supported by advertising, its primary key to success will lie in the sheer number of viewers it can attract.

Similarly a service taking a small margin from sales will be driven to extend the product range to maximise the potential volume of sales. Thus we characterise businesses on this axis using a simple classification – audience aggregation (e.g. portals), product aggregation (e.g. retailers of full or multiple product ranges) and niche marketing (e.g. own product vendors, specialists).

Figure 3.2 below illustrates this axis and highlights another commonly used distinction that reveals a general, though not invariable, characteristic of these services. Services on the left, such as search engines, news summaries and product reviews that steer the customer somewhere else for the complete product, are often referred to as 'navigators', those on the right, where the fulfilment is provided, as 'destination sites'.

Fig. 3.2 The business driver axis describes the key success factor for the service.

The economic buyer – who pays?

The final dimension concerns the real *source of revenue* for the service. Obviously the service can be paid for by either the customer (a typical e-commerce model), or the vendor (either for marketing and support for off-line sales or through commission to a reseller as in auctions). Alternatively it may be supported by a third party (e.g. advertiser-supported services). Once again this is captured in Fig. 3.3 which also draws attention to the intrinsic degree of customer wariness, one simple indication of how hard the service must work to earn the user's trust.

Economic buyer		
Third party pays	Vendor pays	Customer pays
Low ←———	*Customer wariness* ———→	High

Fig. 3.3 The third axis concerns who is paying for the service.

These three dimensions allow us to model what we have come to call the 'Commoditised Internet' in the form of our own 'Revenue Cube' as shown in Fig. 3.4.

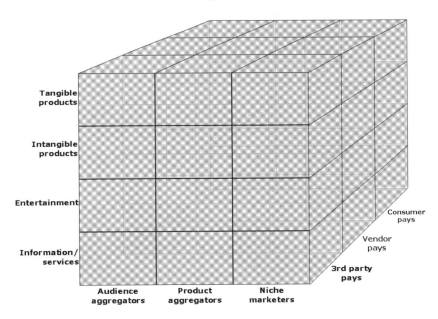

Fig. 3.4 The Revenue Cube: putting the three axes together allows us to build a three-dimensional model of the Commoditised Internet.

Using the Revenue Cube

Most of the prevalent core current business models can be easily and instructively represented within the Revenue Cube, including e-tailers, niche marketers, auctions and exchanges, portals ('true', paid or otherwise[2]), and of course marketing sites.

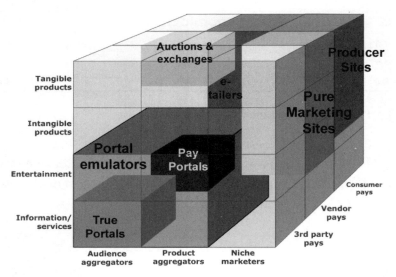

Fig. 3.5 Modelling the prevalent core business models on the Commoditised Internet into the Revenue Cube.

Today's familiar players are also easily mapped into the Cube. Figure 3.6 shows some examples (bear in mind that in such a three-dimensional representation relative size is disguised by perspective).

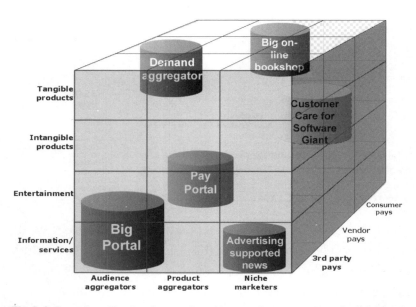

Fig. 3.6 Examples of familiar Commoditised Internet business types in the Revenue Cube.

Many of these players are currently operating more than one business model and therefore, were their full service mapped, they would appear in multiple locations within the cube.

THE PITFALLS OF SIMPLE BUSINESS MODELS

The Revenue Cube is able to map such a wide variety of current digital business propositions because it shares with so many of them a concern only with the products and the mechanics of the transaction. Nowhere, in most formulations of such a business model, is the customer's experience reflected. His or her larger objectives when accessing a service are often only perfunctorily considered.

We contend that this is so – despite constant, brave talk about designing the system around users – because almost all digital services are predicated on maximising the return to the business from the sales of what are, essentially, commodity products and services, or from advertising sales. This is what we call a 'gap-based' approach, providing offerings that meet a simple need and that do not to demand close attention either to the customer's value chain or even to the context in which the need arises.

This state of affairs has arisen in part from misunderstanding of the value opportunity for customers, and in part from attempts to import off-line marketing techniques and tools into an environment where they have proved largely inappropriate. There are, of course, many exceptions to such a broad generalisation; however in this chapter we will first explore the shortcomings of business-model thinking that is based on maximising the return on investment from simple sales.

TOUGH TIMES FOR BUSINESS ON THE COMMODITISED INTERNET

The reverse Midas touch

To explore our concept of the Commoditised Internet in greater depth, we'll look at three of the most common revenue models in today's digital markets. These we can call respectively 'share of product market', 'share of customer spend' and 'share of customer time' (aka the advertising model). Note that there are already some well-known success stories across each of these models. However, with the exception of a small number of skilled and fortunate niche players, the scale of operations of the success stories – the Yahoo!s and Amazons – has been enormous, almost impossibly so.

KEY POINT

The Internet changes everything, they say. Yes. It commoditises everything it touches, with a reverse Midas touch that strips not only cost, but also value, from almost every process.

The dangerous allure of product markets

Businesses seeking a substantial *share of product market* (at first sight perhaps a desirable stance, not least because the view of the Internet as 'just another channel' is an appealing one) are hampered by the price and service transparencies of this near-perfect market. They tend to occupy the corner of the Revenue Cube illustrated in Fig. 3.7.

Some well-known success stories began here: this is where Amazon and Dell started out. Both however have extended the model. Amazon through its expansion into music, games, software and gifts is seeking to leverage its initial success into a stake in our next model, *share of customer spend* (see below), and Dell is arguably aiming to use the sale of computer peripherals to the same end.

Applying Michael Porter's[3] generic competitive strategies to explore the effects of major Internet drivers on product markets,

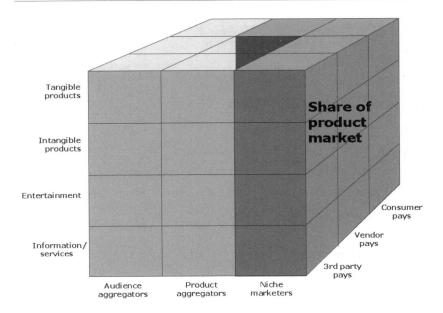

Fig. 3.7 Using the Revenue Cube to identify product market business models.

we can see how three of the four potential approaches hold little promise in digital markets.

Cost advantage

Cost leadership, where establishing the lowest possible costs of operation confers competitive advantage, is forced on product marketers whose Internet objectives lie in geographic and socio-demographic reach, pursuit of incremental sales and product market control. Since price transparency creates the requirement to match or better the lowest offer, decreasing margins are available, with the result that enormous scale of operation is required to reach a point of comfort. This is a refuge that is still continually under threat from the very transparency that it seeks to benefit from.

Many of the now defunct dot-com start-ups either aimed at this model (believing that the absence of physical stores automatically conferred cost advantages) or, discovering the consequences of reduced geographical barriers, found themselves there any-way.

Not that this is out of reach to all players but, by definition, the competitive risks to those seeking market control are high and do not much diminish with the achievement of apparent success or over time. And the scale required to reach a broad target mar-ket means that a valuable and sustainable space in the market can be occupied profitably by very few participants. Thus the (now highly questionable) claim, that being first to market is critical to achieving success with these business models.

Does a narrower target market help?

Unfortunately, even where the offer is targeted on a sector of the market rather than the broad mass, many of the same problems arise. The reduction of geographical barriers increases competi-tion in all sectors, once again decreasing the available margin and increasing the required scale wherever cost becomes the primary focus.

The pursuit of operational efficiency

Cost advantages are also sought via digital channels through an-other and more widely embraced approach: the application of In-ternet technology to the incremental cost reduction of basic op-erational activities. Many business-to-business applications of the Internet focus in this area, often directed at the supply chain or at redrawing company boundaries, especially through new ways to outsource functions. However, the changes are as likely to take the form of proprietary internal process development or redevelop-ment as to involve participation in public markets.

This, the e-business approach, which may have no discern-ible impact on the customer interface, is in fact no longer a strate-gic choice: it is a necessity for most businesses. Like the majority of generic improvements to operational efficiency, the option is open to all, and failure to pursue it results in progressive erosion of competitive position. But, like all such improvements, it rapidly reaches the point of diminishing returns[4] (though these limits are not yet reached in many industries and the transformation has some way to run).

In many ways the most successful cost advantage gains achieved through business efficiency strategies – those that have impacted the customer experience the most – are the demand-management practices operated by, or as an outlet for, many businesses with high fluctuating demand or perishable products or services. Thus, trading in reduced-price airline tickets or holidays has appeal to both the bargain-seeking customer and the business that is trying to manage its inventory. But note that, however successful these services can be, they are seldom central to the business proposition of the originating companies concerned.

Differentiation advantage

Differentiation, where either a demonstrably superior offer, or a stronger brand (or, of course, ideally a combination of both) confers high perceived value on the product, in turn enabling a higher price, is savagely attacked by the transparency of digital markets. One could argue that to expect this strategy to work effectively in what is – by necessity – a commodity and commoditising environment is simply not good sense. When a buyer can not only shop around with relative ease for the best fixed or demand-managed prices (using product-aggregation services such as MySimon), but also participate in one of the many on-line auctions, reverse auctions or demand-aggregation sites (such as Letsbuyit.com), the very value that underpins the strategy is slashed. The customer is continually refocused on price as the primary consideration, and the paucity of links with the context for use, or support for the larger purpose with which the purchase is associated, undermines the opportunity to emphasise value-adding features.

Perhaps more subtly, and certainly in the case of, for example, luxury consumer goods, a sizeable portion of the value associated by the consumer with the product is the elegance and personal touch embodied in the purchasing process itself. This we see enshrined on New Bond Street, Madison Avenue and Rodeo Drive. The small numbers of consumers who can afford these products have little incentive to spend their money in such a cold, service-light, commodity environment. (To prove the point, there have been some high-profile casualties in this area, most notably Boo.com.)

More importantly in terms of this discussion, the same transparency can seriously erode the essential cachet and standing of a Gucci, a Prada or a Zegna. These are not brands of the people!

Focused differentiation

Finally, focused differentiation, where a targeted offer is precisely tailored for a section of the market rather than the whole, puts customer knowledge and specialisation at the core of the proposition, bringing us much closer to the value we seek on-line.

Note immediately how our touchstones of meaning and trust are far happier when the information that is on offer is provided within a context that is focused, credible and clearly committed to the service of a distinct customer need. This is a market that expects to pay some premium for having its needs met more precisely than commodity or mass-marketed brands are likely to achieve, and that brings existing knowledge and understanding, generally creating a meaningful context for the offer.

(Note also though that mass customisation – where a range of product options supposedly caters for the different needs of different markets – fails to realise these outcomes. Being focused narrowly on a product and failing to address the critical issue of the customer's broader purpose (the focus of our next chapter) mass customisation rapidly returns us to a cost competitive environment.)

That proviso aside, as we move on from the current problems to examining potential solutions, we'll find that the focus model contains many elements of what we perceive to be the successful digital strategies of the future and that it plays an important role in returning value to more broadly differentiated products.

The crisis of loyalty

We talked in a previous chapter about the crisis of loyalty, how the promiscuous customer is devoid of the sentimental attachments that the misguided marketer seeks in digital markets.

This does not bode well at all for our second model, *share of customer spend*. As with share of product market, the initial allure and the apparent simplicity of the model are beguiling. Share of spend in the digital domain is likely to be engineered by way of migration from a position of strength in a product market, across to contiguous product and service categories, leveraging established customer trust and loyalty along the way. This has been a popular approach with financial service companies going on-line, appearing to mirror their standard direct marketing efforts. Most retailers have also instinctively adopted it. It's in many respects a classic 1:1 play, with the other key element being the much-discussed and perhaps overrated 'brand permission', that theoretically enables the shift across to new product or service types. Business models on the World Wide Web that aim to achieve share of customer spend occupy the sectors of the Revenue Cube illustrated in Fig. 3.8.

But without a meaningful and trustworthy service context, within which these extended e-commerce offerings can achieve relevant connections with customer purpose and the tasks in hand, the attempt to extend and cluster such category offerings under a CRM umbrella stands a high chance of failure. In an environment where brand and the convenience of proximity as vehicles for product selection lack the teeth they have enjoyed off-line, and where both meaning and trust are likely to be, if anything, eroded by hasty attempts to stretch them across into new markets, a share of cus-

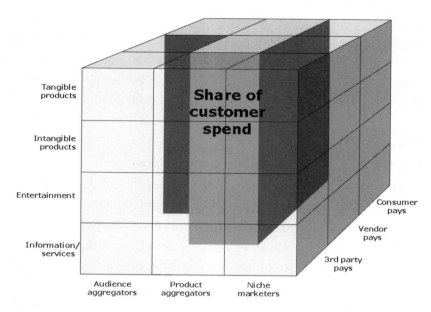

Fig. 3.8 The sectors of the Revenue Cube occupied by businesses seeking share of customer spend.

tomer spend model surely carries unreasonable risk. And, as with the share of product market approach, it is hard to fight the generic focus on price; with the inevitable consequence that while loss leaders and flagship products may get bought, the cross-selling of more profitable lines has to surmount even higher hurdles than usual.

Sorry, no time...

Exploiting *customer time* (or, if you like, the customer eyeball) through the adoption of the *advertising model*,[5] as has been done with some success by both large and smaller specialised portals (from Yahoo! to UKPlus), is an option that will certainly retain some credibility in tomorrow's digital markets, although seldom in isolation. We believe that those who succeed with this approach will be businesses who venture beyond the customer aggregation model, to make available valuable tools and services, especially tools for networking with other users, and for the restructuring of generic tasks, such as shared diary management and file storage.

Increasingly, even within the largest of these concerns, the requirement is to segment the audience and provide focused information and service offers, as they seek to sustain value for the customer.

Those businesses that seek to stretch the advertising model beyond its natural home in audience (and to a lesser degree product) aggregation will continue to be less successful. Attempts have been made to stretch the model to provide at least some revenue contribution across wide swathes of the Revenue Cube (as Fig. 3.9 shows), often with little benefit to the bottom line, as niche content owners have discovered. (Indeed in the rush to get a piece of the 'portal pie', even small retail sites tried to benefit from selling advertising space, and many tried to reverse the process, letting others do the actual selling while they charged for space and took a cut. The list of dot-com disasters is littered with hybrid models, which sought to combine some advertising revenue with a small margin on incidental product sales made as a result of click-through to a transaction site.)

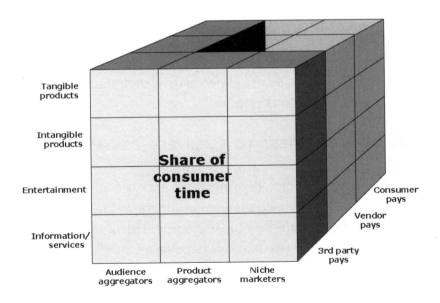

Fig. 3.9 Sectors of the Revenue Cube that business models based on share of customer time have sought to occupy.

Whatever their other objectives, businesses grounded in this model will need to accept that severely flawed concepts such as 'stickiness', where valuable busy customers (who apparently have nothing better to do!) are persuaded to loiter in the space soaking up targeted brand messages, simply erode meaning, trust, value and ultimately loyalty.

This is really 'old-marketing think', whose applicability outside digital markets may rest intact – albeit reduced in scale – but whose adoption inside them is fatal. Our valuable customers have very little time to spare, and that time is increasingly perceived by them as precious, and also as under threat from businesses and their willing participation in – and indeed promotion of – the bewildering information explosion.

Another serious blow to the advertiser model has yet to reveal itself fully. This is the coming rapid contraction (following the current explosion in channel and device availability) in opportunities for brand encounter in digital markets, as an increasing range and number of important service functions become automated. This, as we will be exploring in later chapters, is becoming a primary driver of future value provision to the customer and, as complexity grows, a critical necessity if digital markets are to usefully extend their function.

TRENDS IN BUSINESS-TO-BUSINESS (B2B) MARKETS

To concentrate on differentiating the business-to-business from consumer markets in the digital environment will not cast a great deal of additional light on our discussion. However, it is worth pointing out that the two markets have developed along parallel tracks and perhaps it is no surprise that they have had to learn similar lessons, albeit in a very different order. In many ways the business marketplace has had to learn faster. From the perspective of our discussion, several interesting developments in these business markets offer clear pointers as to the problems encountered, and the more successful responses point the way in which digital businesses must move if they are to be successful.

The erosion of margins by the exchange model ...

The first of these lessons has been the rapid discovery that merely providing efficient exchanges that reduce transaction costs, like Bizbuyer.com, is not in itself an adequate incentive for participation. A corollary of this is the tendency for such models to disadvantage the supplier side, generating further barriers to participation and thus making the achievement of critical mass and liquidity – and with them profitability – harder. This is significant in that it illustrates one logical end-point for consumer markets too: if supplier margins are eroded too far, no suppliers will want to participate.

... and also by the emergence of peer-to-peer trading

A related outcome has been that, as competition between exchanges pushes the available fee for their use down, the achievement of profitability based on a margin of the transaction alone is becoming close to impossible. Moreover, as many ventures are realising, peer-to-peer capability allows businesses to perform simple volume- and price-based transactions without need of the services of an exchange. There is a business in assisting companies to do this, but it is a very different one from the operation of an exchange. As we shall see, it is increasingly the case that customers can perform these transactions too: marketplaces *per se* become redundant when the buyer can simplify the process, and in all probability save money, by going direct.

Public exchanges go private ...

Further major lessons for business markets have been that relationships are central, the selection of goods that are sufficiently commoditised to be traded between anonymous parties is very limited, and trust is critical. Consequently, the major corporates, who would contribute most liquidity to public exchanges, have tended to form Virtual Private Networks instead, where approved partners and suppliers can collaborate more closely and openly than in public services. Public business-to-business exchanges have thus found themselves forced to radically change their own models, providing extensive collaborative features to ensure continued custom.

... and collaboration services come to the fore

The last relevant lesson lies in the discovery that it is in the provision of supporting services to enable collaborative relationships, control of quality and the reduction of risk, that much of the real value to participants is to be found. Biztro.com for instance provides back-office support, including human resource management applications, for small business as well as helping with their procurement needs. Thus support for collaborative product development, market specific expertise and brokerage services become critically important on the one hand, and provision for forward-buying, hedging and options on the other. Indeed some of the most outstanding successes in business-to-business markets have been achieved in the market for collaborative services, such as co-development, and remote project management tools, like ProjectPlace.com.

Again this echoes consumer markets in which, as we have indicated above, the most promising way forward seems to lie in providing facilities within a context that is focused, credible and clearly committed to the service of a distinct customer need.

As a final sting in the tail, it is worth mentioning that, having grasped the real importance of content, business-to-business markets have had to learn rather more quickly than consumer ones that it is not merely volume but relevance, adequacy and trustworthiness that matters to users.

THE CONSISTENT FRUSTRATION OF CUSTOMER PURPOSE

With the obvious exceptions of their engagement with certain entertainment-based models (and also excluding those few remaining customers whose pure fascination with the medium leads them to spend huge amounts of time on-screen ...) valuable customers in digital markets are primarily focused upon solving problems, and thus upon finding simple, effective, trustworthy resources that conveniently and unobtrusively support the unique and personal purposes that emerge from those needs. Recent research tends to bear this out: as Fig. 3.10 shows, customers arrive primarily with a specific task, often an information-based one, in mind.

KEY POINT

Customers, in other words, mainly turn to digital markets to perform sequences of tasks. They will assign trust, loyalty and ultimately the rewards of success to those environments that meaningfully support these tasks, across the widest range of their potential needs within the overall area of interest.

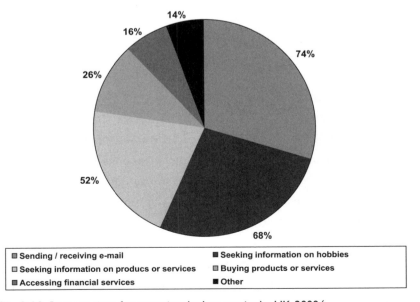

□ Sending / receiving e-mail ■ Seeking information on hobbies
□ Seeking information on producs or services □ Buying products or services
■ Accessing financial services ■ Other

Fig. 3.10 Reasons given for accessing the Internet in the UK, 2000.[6]

'Silo Syndrome' – the core of the customer's problem

Holding in mind this focus on purpose and task, from the customer point of view the most severe obstruction to value in digital markets is the chronic fragmentation of service offerings across not only their own purpose, but also across business and revenue models and channels and devices.

'Information wants to be free'... and by golly it's made it!

One of the more ironic digital success stories is that information – the very raw material of digital value – is largely free on the Commoditised Internet.

The original promise of hypertext conjured up an academic's dream, the vision of an infinite global library. But in the real marketplace, customers are drowning. Information is – at least from a commercial point of view – currently worse than worthless: the typical experience of researching even the most simple subject or requirement on-line is a highly dissociative one, leaving the customer feeling at the same time over-informed and full of doubt.

What's happening here?

Go back again to our focused customer.

KEY POINT

Information in this sense creates work for the customer. Problems are not solved; they are in fact enlarged, increased by information.

We see immediately that all this information often has less than zero value because it is, almost without exception, available in a manner that is entirely divorced from the all-important context of the customer's purpose and task.

The outcome has been that only five or six Web sites currently support the majority of customer's information access habits. Customers, it seems, would rather struggle through the mass of generic information on a portal and the complexities of, at least partly, personalising it than perform the work of investigating (and establish the credibility of) a wider range of services that may be more tailored to their needs.

Other than the giant portals, those few content businesses that are currently profitable in digital markets are – exclusively, as far as we know – those that are able to incorporate their information into the purposes and tasks of a valuable customer set. They are integrated into the key working processes of the customer, providing a key service with a very high 'time value'.[7]

The crowded landscape of new devices

At the time of writing, a week rarely passes without the launch of a new access device. If you're reading this book you'll need no reminder of this! But there are some questionable assumptions about access that need rigorous challenging.

What happens to the experience of the focused customer when tasks become spread across a series of non-contiguous environments? We might initially argue that the proliferation of devices increases customer control, while at the same time in-

---

AND BACK IN THE REAL WORLD ...

A November 2000 report by high-tech consultants Strategy Analytics observed that, by the end of that year, 52 million US homes, or 50 percent of the total, would have an Internet PC, and 6.3 million (six percent) would own one or more online appliances (interactive TVs, online games consoles, or Web terminals). In contrast, even by 2005, barely half of the online terminals in European homes will be PCs. In fact, currently only 39.8 million European homes – 26 percent of the total – own an Internet PC. However, 21.5 million of the total (or 14 percent) own an online appliance. In fact, the leading online appliance market is the UK, with 30 percent household penetration, followed by France (16 percent) and Spain (15 percent).

Strategy Analytics, 'Windows on the Web: The Market for Internet and Online Appliances', 2000.

---

creasing value-adding opportunities for business. So what's the problem?

Well, it's simple. Once the fascination with today's plethora of widgetry wears off (and let's not pretend that this isn't exactly what happens) and customers start to look for real day-to-day value in the applications they use, the experience of jumping across different channels and devices in order to perform basic sets of tasks changes from a jolly experiment to a fragmented inconvenience.

Silos of activity, with little continuity between them across the purpose and the 'task set'[8] actually prohibit value and trust-building contact – and what's more, no meaningful customer contact cycle can be established and maintained. In other words, nobody wins.

'Island-hopping' between business models

The traditional model of attraction in the Commoditised Internet assumed that we would guide the customer through an ever-more-focused experience, beginning possibly with a search,

---

AND BACK IN THE REAL WORLD…

According to a November 2000 study by the Boston Consulting Group, one in four owners of mobile devices stops using m-commerce applications after the first few attempts. However, most people surveyed expected these services to play an important role in their future daily lives.

82 percent of current and potential users think that the mobile device will become their personal travel assistant within the next three years, and 61 percent expect these devices to become universal payment tools.

Mobile Commerce: Winning the On-Air Customer, Boston Consulting Group, November 2000.

---

thence into a specialised content environment and thence, through perhaps an expert system supporting product and service specification, towards a purchase.

But this assumes that the paradigm matches typical customer purposes and tasks. And as is so often the case, the model has largely been defined by the limitations of what it has been technically possible to achieve in linking sequential or, harder still, discontinuous tasks.

On one hand, the main problem faced by potentially valuable niche offers is that they are unable to occupy in isolation a convincing spread of the task set that reflects customer mode and purpose. They rely considerably upon the context provided by broader offerings (for example, portals and vortals) through which they can with luck achieve a certain degree of customer relevance. But if, as we'll see below, those larger contexts are unable to fit comfortably with customer purpose and task, the chances for the niche player to be in 'the right place at the right time' to create optimal and timely value for the customer and achieve a sale are severely diminished.

Portals, at the other extreme (and most of what are called 'vortals'), have the reverse problem. They represent a glut of information and are therefore typically unable to create value by linking easily in with specific customer purpose. Being paradoxically both information-friendly and customer-hostile, they create hard work for the customer, which is only indirectly and with effort supportive of the execution of the task set in hand.

So our customer is, if you like, reduced to a kind of wearisome 'island-hopping' across a sea of largely useless information, between tiny islands of value. Or, to get back onto dry land, a little like being compelled to walk to work in a never-ending game of hopscotch!

WHERE WILL THE VALUE COME FROM?

So in the context of the Commoditised Internet, it's tough for more than a small number of businesses to sustainably create either customer value or shareholder returns in digital markets.

Margins, loyalty and customer time are under an increasing squeeze, while simultaneously the customer experience is typically fragmented, dissonant, and despite an apparently endless flood of technical innovation, very light on meaning, trust and value. Customer needs, and the vast majority of current offerings in today's digital markets, simply don't seem to speak the same language.

TO SUMMARISE

- The Commoditised Internet offers little comfort for both business and its customer: customers seek support for their purposes and tasks in vain, and the nature of the environment erodes all sources of sustainable competitive advantage for business.
- This has been reflected by recent dramatic contractions on both the demand and supply sides of the digital business.
- Value for both sides is now clearly to be sought in new models of service and trade.

NOTES

1   An issue we explore more deeply in Chapter 5, 'Meaning, Trust and Value'.
2   Many of what are dubbed portals, are in fact – in varied degrees of comprehensiveness and credibility – destinations that are typically funded by a product or service supplier attempting to offer 'compelling content' as a loyalty-generation device. We call these 'portal emulators'.

3   Michael E. Porter, *Competitive Advantage*, Free Press, New York, 1985.

4   Gary Hamel, *Leading the Revolution*, Harvard Business School Press, 2000.

5   As explored in detail in Chapter 5, 'Meaning, Trust and Value'.

6   Thebuzz@netprofit, Issue 10, Net Profit Publications.

7   'Time value' here means the value of information in the context of its enabling a rapid reaction to, typically, opportunity or risk.

8   A sequence of tasks demanded by the customer's purposive activity.

CHAPTER 4

Modes, Purposes and Tasks

'Take care of the sense and the sounds will take care of themselves.'

IN THIS CHAPTER WE LOOK AT

- customer experience and expectation in digital markets in greater depth;
- the problem of interruptive marketing techniques;
- the *paradox of mode*, a critical insight into customer needs and the delivery of value;
- the concept of customer mode, and its three components;
- customer purposes and types of task; and
- the cycle of customer engagement from mode through to integration.

THE PARADOX OF CUSTOMER MODE

A profoundly intimate, wholly impersonal encounter

The customer encounter with the business in digital markets is, as we've said, uniquely intimate. Yet at the very same time it's ice cold and impersonal! We make a promise for our product or service and the customer in digital markets will hold us to it more tenaciously and to-the-letter than the most obsessive offline customer ever would.

KEY POINT

The customer is simultaneously highly sensitive to the degree of value that's being delivered, and uninterested in any kind of emotional bond with the business.

When we get this wrong, the intimacy of the encounter makes itself felt (just as when we have a rude or unhelpful encounter in a shop), and the promiscuous customer turns on the business. We've wasted her time, betrayed her precious trust, or possibly just confused her a little with a bewildering interface.

At the same time, the neutrality of the environment – you might even call it a kind of 'amorality' – enables her to calmly assassinate our brand without the slightest concern, before turning away. (Notice how much less likely it would be for this to happen so rapidly in a physical, personal encounter with the business, where social rules, manners and custom would tend to preclude this type of extreme, terminal reaction.)

What customers don't want

Why is that? Don't these people know the meaning of the word patience? Can't they see how much better the digital service is, even with the odd glitch, compared with the old one?

We think the answer here is generally yes, they do and they can. But the truth is that – perhaps alarmingly – in digital markets, the promiscuous customer generally doesn't really care that much. The emotional buffers, and also the low service expecta-

WALKING THE TALK

Janet has been trying to get an email response from ChemiKit.com – a supplier of classroom and laboratory equipment – for some days now regarding a query she has about the safety of a particular piece of laboratory equipment. She is concerned about introducing the kit to the class project we mentioned earlier until this issue is cleared up.

Despite the fact that the interface of the ChemiKit.com Web site is warm and welcoming, and also that they send Janet regular (not always useful or relevant) marketing messages by email, their customer service is not responding nearly fast enough to her in this case.

This sets up a considerable dissonance … on the one hand she's hearing how important her custom is to them, and being solicited regularly with new offers, and on the other, the behaviour of the firm clearly contradicts these apparently good intentions.

This is like asking a customer the question, 'What can we do for you today, Janet?' and then turning away and ignoring the response. It immediately erodes any of the minimal brand loyalty that has been accrued and it's very likely that, despite her good nature, Janet may use one or more of the discussion groups to which she belongs to vent her frustration, thereby doing a lot more damage to potential ChemiKit business and the firm's reputation in the academic community.

tions that fostered the customer's tolerance and patience in the Golden Years of Terrible Service are fading here. There's little or no direct human contact to support bonding; the customer's experience of quality in one environment automatically raises the bar for all other digital players. The promiscuous customer knows that we have no choice but to take no for an answer, again and again, until perhaps one day she says yes.

Remember that the role of CRM here needs careful placing. Unlike the business, this customer isn't sitting in front of the screen agonising about how to evolve his loyalty to the supplier, how to get closer to the company … This customer's loyalty is, if anything, perhaps to the digital environment as a whole, and conceivably over time to certain of the spaces that are forming in the environment. This customer may indeed be in love with being digital.

But he'll continue to withhold the affection and loyalty – indeed any form of emotional engagement – which our misguided sentimental marketer craves. Until we accept that fact, our stance in digital markets will remain low in critical relevance and toxically high in intrusive, inappropriate offerings.

How to add value by getting out of the way

The loneliness of the long-distance customer

The current proliferation of smaller mobile devices supports our customer in the performance of an ever-growing range of important – often tiny – day-to-day tasks. These tasks, where they occur in the commercial environment, would often previously have been performed – or at least assisted – by a representative of the business.

We have often assumed that the automated delivery of this value, without human involvement from the supplier, in some sense represented a new and superior kind of value to the customer (e.g. through 24/7 access, a greater range of options and preferences) and value to the business (e.g. through cost savings, customer data capture, etc.).

But personal customer service in any form outside digital markets builds value and loyalty in a fashion that we cannot duplicate on the screen. The off-line collaboration with the supplier to solve the customer's problem, whatever form it may take, has always been time-consuming and costly. But let's not ignore the value-add derived from the satisfaction of some simple human

A BETTER PUBLIC ADDRESS SYSTEM ...

When Federal Express launched its on-line package-tracking service for customers in the mid-90s, it was hailed as a considerable step forward, one of the earlier examples of a genuinely useful Web-based service. Technically, the company achieved this facility by opening up a Web-based window into an existing and thoroughly tested aspect of their own internal systems. In other words, a relatively straightforward piece of work that has surely saved the company many millions of dollars since its introduction.

And they went on to build on this initiative rapidly, introducing a range of value-adding software functions – mostly usable on or downloadable from the Web – that created real customer loyalty, by simply making customer tasks much easier to perform.

But we need to ask what happened to the personal contact between customers and staff that this new facility replaced. Did this track-it-yourself function introduce a chilliness to the previously quite warm and personal brand experience of the FedEx customer? And, by the way, if the company's service promise of 'The World On Time' was to be carried through onto the Web, why would we even need to track our own packages – don't you do that for us?

needs – to communicate, to feel part of things, to make contact, and also perhaps to share the responsibility for consequences.

Our engagement with the on-line marketplace is therefore not simply a transposed version of the off-line experience. We are social beings, and promiscuous customers are strikingly alone in their excursions into digital markets.

How marketing messages can attack meaning, trust and value
The increase in control, access and apparent choice experienced by the promiscuous customer renders the intrusion of any irrelevant or

HE SAID ... SHE SAID ...

'To create the value (what customers like) there must be emotional connectivity between the front-line person and the customer. It is not enough for a front-line person to smile, say the right things and try to be enthusiastic. The connection will only be made if they are sensitive to each customer's individual requirements for emotional value. Sometimes a smile and enthusiasm are totally inappropriate. Without emotional connectivity at a personal level there is a high risk that a customer will defect. This applies especially if the customer has little emotional attachment to the brand.'

David Freemantle, *What Customers Like About You*, Nicholas Brealey Publishing, 1998.

'All our research shows this direct relationship: The more shopper-employee contacts that take place, the greater the average sale. Talking with an employee has a way of drawing a customer in closer.

Paco Underhill, *Why We Buy – The Science of Shopping*, Orion Business Books, 1999.

inappropriate marketing messages highly interruptive. In fact, any 'off-mode' experience with the brand has a similarly erosive effect.

The arrival of a pop-up 'did you know?' or 'how about ...?' message in the customer's attention space – no matter how theoretically helpful or potentially relevant it might be in the mind of the business – is almost always distracting and dissonant. It breaks the flow of the work being performed (and note that this experience of 'flow' is one of the few pleasures left to the promiscuous customer in the screen environment!).

Moving back out of digital markets, would we ever deliberately refuse, or make inaccessible, a basic service to a valuable customer, while at one and the same time bombarding them with unwanted and, for them, irrelevant marketing messages?

I'M SORRY ... YOU'RE GOING TO HAVE TO READ OUR MISSION STATEMENT

Visions and missions are everywhere in the customer's eye line at the moment, as if by their very presence they bring some sort of extra meaning or comfort to the experience offered by the business – a starchy form of corporate soul-baring, perhaps. Remember when every Web site kicked off with a word from the chairman or CEO, and you were exhorted to 'read our mission statement'?

OK, no serious harm done, certainly back in the days when just accessing a site successfully was a cause for celebration ... But this underlying need to embed those messages everywhere in the customer encounter lives on, in the form of that extra click you have to make to get past a promotional item, that extra field that needs filling in before you can get at the service you really came for and, of course, alongside your bank balance on the screen, the offer (at a cost of no small download time, as the usability folks would tut) of a service you probably already signed up for ...

Blind to the clamour of full-colour billboards and deaf to shrill TV ads, if I can't easily access my bank balance by (say) phone or PDA when I expect to, I'm unhappy. My bank has deprived me of essential value and instantly leaked a lot of my already meagre store of loyalty.

THE PARADOX OF MODE

At this level in digital markets, less is invariably more. And this is the basis for what we call 'the paradox of mode'.

When developing businesses in digital markets therefore, it is essential that we focus, above and before all

KEY POINT

The more restricted the environment (e.g. the smaller and more mobile the access device) and the more specific and day-to-day the task to be performed, the higher the pressure on the brand, and the greater the threat to customer meaning, trust, value and loyalty.

else, upon those encounters where the promiscuous customer is looking to perform the most apparently mundane, low-impact, unexciting tasks. Prior to that, everything else is, sadly, the most extreme form of cant and must be unceremoniously thrown out.

The modal approach to building customer value

Far from consigning the user experience work to the far end of a project (where the more generic principles of usability are of course highly important in terms of the quality of the customer experience), businesses in digital markets need to stop worrying about how to put the customer at the centre of the business (remember, she doesn't want to be there anyway!). Instead, they should start focusing hard on *building services that place the customer's infinitely variable modes, and the tasks that are derived from these modes, at the centre of the business.*

What is mode?

Customer mode in digital markets is defined and determined by three closely linked elements:

- the time, location and cultural circumstances of the customer (which we call the *environmental* element of mode);
- the context – the point of arrival or the previous environment – or task set – from which the customer arrives at the space (which we call the *contextual* element of mode);
- the intent with which a customer approaches or enters a market space (which we call the *purposive* element of mode);

A CLOSER LOOK AT ENVIRONMENTAL MODE

Environmental mode may initially be explored by examining the customer's pattern of activity and the locations in which he may be found during a typical day.

Figure 4.1 captures this for the most generic case.

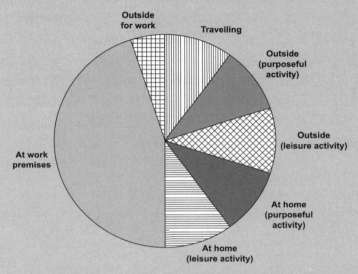

Fig. 4.1 A generic activity pattern showing where the customer might be found during a typical working day

The activity pattern revealed allows some predictions to be made about likely channels and devices the customer will choose to use for establishing contact.

For example, the most likely modes of contact for a customer who is taking a break from shopping will be the mobile phone or PDA whereas, in the office, a PC is more likely and from home perhaps interactive television.

The influence of culture

A further aspect of environmental mode is linked to the cultural conditions that apply. Both national cultures and peer-group influences

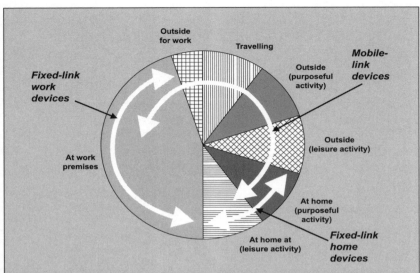

Fig. 4.2 The effect of location and activity on choice of channel and device.

may affect the primary channel of communication. An example of this is the current heavy use by teenagers of the SMS facilities on mobile telephones, which would make these favoured devices for many services, overriding issues of suitability of the interface.

Culture also influences content. It has been a long-standing sin of Web designers to assume that, magically and without question, their audience shares the same cultural context. Even attacking the problem of global communication with expert translation solves only part of the problem. To use a perhaps trivial example, if I want to connect with local sports fans in New Zealand or in the UK, Michael Jordan is probably, despite his extraordinary fame, the wrong name to use. I need references to Jonah Lomu or David Beckham. (Mr Jordan is actually better known to children than to mature fans outside his home court, due in part to his movie career.)

More subtly, culture may affect the nature of the tasks associated with particular goals and the way in which these are carried out. To assume a one-size-fits-all navigation structure may risk confusing – even offending – customers who are unfamiliar with the underlying cultural assumptions.

A CLOSER LOOK AT CONTEXTUAL MODE

There are several aspects of customer context that may be examined. If the customer is already on-line, for instance, the site they originate from may provide useful clues. If I'm looking to acquire software to meet a particular business requirement, I might arrive in a new digital environment (leaving aside for a moment which channel or device I might be using) that is managed by a specialist vendor, via a content or expert advice environment, into which I came, in turn, via some form of search mechanism. The context from which I have emerged provides many clues as to my overall purpose and enables the planning of a generally clear and limitable selection of offers that could be of relevance to me.

Similarly, where a service is associated with known or researchable patterns of off-line activity, the nature of the tasks being performed provides contextual information about likely needs and the available access to touchpoints.

Figure 4.3 explores the balance of activities during a working day for a typical manager, showing the tasks she could be involved in. These will be associated with services she might need and the touchpoints through which she will expect them to be delivered. Such analysis, undertaken in the context of the intended service, will provide some of the most accurate guidance available to customers' needs and wants and how they might expect solutions to be delivered.

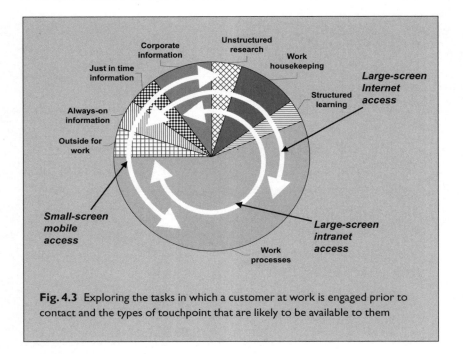

Fig. 4.3 Exploring the tasks in which a customer at work is engaged prior to contact and the types of touchpoint that are likely to be available to them

The challenge of purposive mode

Information about customers' contextual mode may allow us to make limited deductions about their intent based on the activities they are performing when they arrive, but there is little we can positively know in advance about the purposive element of mode.

Yet this is the most important of the three modal conditions; it dictates the tasks customers will need to perform and is the major determinant of whether they perceive the service to be relevant to their needs.

Purposive mode embraces a wide range of needs, wants and expectations and it unfolds into a range of key, important (and possibly contributory) tasks. It can be revealed only through thorough understanding and detailed research of the market and empathetic creation of scenarios. Its full range is iteratively unfolded in combination with task analysis, which is examined later in this chapter.

Taken together, information about these three elements of customer mode allows their expectations to be anticipated in the process of the assembly of the digital space, to maximise the value that can be delivered as relevant service.

KEY POINT

The degree to which substantial commercial offerings in digital markets are able to deliver real value to the customer is heavily 'gated' by their ability to meet these modes – which necessitate a sequence of one or more cohesive tasks in a context of desirable services types and channels – with the relevant services that customers expect.

How the elements of mode play out for the customer

Broadly speaking, the contextual element will combine with the purposive element to determine the nature and range of responses that could optimally meet a customer's current need. The environmental element will contribute substantially to the selection of channel and device.

Note that the environmental element can in some instances override the other two, in the sense that a user may wish to access information or services – perhaps in an emergency – using a device that may in terms of the nature of the service or the information type be less than ideal.

> **AND BACK IN THE REAL WORLD ...**
>
> AOL has consistently succeeded in massaging its customer loyalty upwards by supporting daily tasks such as diary management and stock portfolio tracking. This is true 'stickiness', where real value brings customers back to the AOL environment to perform tasks that have direct relevance to their day-to-day lives.

MODE IN ACTION

At the time of writing, the network infrastructure publicly available – certainly in the US and Europe – is still developing (while in, for example, Hong Kong and Singapore, high-bandwidth always-on services are becoming commonplace). However, the range of currently popular devices gives us enough leeway to create a useful example of the interplay between the three elements of mode.

Mode and context

Janet enters a section of a medical advice Web site, having learned of the site's existence (and its possible usefulness in terms of her son Rocky's well-being) in one of the regular personalised email bulletins she receives on the subject of food allergies and anaphylaxis. In this case, given that the email bulletin – from where she 'arrived' onto the Web site having clicked on an embedded link – is probably a reasonably well-trusted resource for Janet, the following can be assumed to be the case:

- She already knows a little about the overall site, and also knows what to expect in that she has deliberately selected the embedded link on the basis of it being of particular interest to her. This means that a huge amount of introductory material, or indeed credentials, may be useful for her to have available if needed, but she could find them obtrusive if they must be waded through to get to the good stuff.
- She is conceivably either a concerned parent or medical professional whose understanding of the larger issues surrounding food allergies may already be considerable. So again she will most likely wish to cut to the key issues (where meaning, in this case, resides for a customer like Janet), rather than engage with introductory material.

- Despite her familiarity with the subject matter and the adequate credibility of the bulletin that introduced Janet to this site, as the concerned parent of a child with a serious allergy, trust and credibility will remain constant issues – this is literally life or death for Janet and her family. Thus the appropriate certifications will need to be visibly at hand throughout her encounter.
- We can also assume that, having deliberately clicked on an embedded link to access a Web site, Janet is using a device that is comfortably capable of displaying that site, i.e. a PC, laptop or similar, with reasonable bandwidth.

Mode and purpose

Janet's initial purpose – which may of course rapidly evolve in a range of possible directions, contingent upon her experience in this environment – is to explore recent developments in treatments for the potentially fatal anaphylactic shock.

- A sadly common practice in the Commoditised Internet is to immediately apply this knowledge, not to develop for Janet a focused and personally relevant experience, but to throw up premature and intrusive product offerings ('GOTCHA!' – 'We know what YOU'RE after, Janet!') in the form of banners and – arguably a little less destructive – personalised selections of text links in the navigation areas of the page. Meaning and trust go out the window straight away, and surely it's clear that for this customer, with this purpose and this degree of emotional attachment to the subject matter, such manipulation of the experience is going to be highly dissociative.
- What we need to do in the face of what we understand Janet's purpose to be (and that may be an imperfect understanding) is to steer clear of any product or service solicitations for now and

focus on setting the foundations for her meaningful and trust-worthy initial encounter with the space. How is this done? For example, by (assuming we're talking about a relatively standard Web site produced at the time of writing) making a prominently available shortlist of the most frequently-used links around the subject matter (no, not right across the whole range of medical science, just in the field of allergy!). At the same time, since none of these may fit the bill, a broader range of options should also be to hand, including some form of focused search function.

- It's likely that Janet will appreciate some form of shortlisting function, since she will be exploring and assessing a range of information for relevance. In addition, she's likely to want to print one or more selections for later reading off-line.

- Again, Janet's purposive mode impacts the likely device she's using, and again we can assume that a PC or laptop is in use, and as mentioned above, she will quite possibly be looking for easy and rapid (low-graphic) printing.

- Each of these considerations opens up a distinct sequence of tasks – the 'task set' – that is logically derived from Janet's initial (and unfolding) purpose. She may, for example, decide (having first crossed the necessary thresholds of meaning and trust) to purchase a recent report on the condition that interests her. She may alternatively wish only to register for news updates on the subject. More substantially, she may wish to make contact with a specialist practitioner in the field. Each of these options demands a very different set of functions, the customer expectations are equally diverse, and – not to be understated here – the offering of these various products or services requires the site to have in place either an owned resource or a reliable partnership with another supplier.

- Note also that, despite the core device being almost certainly, as we mentioned above, a PC or laptop, Janet may wish to have a consultant contact her by mobile phone, have selected important news updates sent to her as text messages on the same phone, or choose to participate at some later time in an online conference using the higher-bandwidth facilities at the school.

Mode and environment

Relatively simple in contrast is the issue of environmental mode. Looking at the customer's environment – their likely location and the time of day – we can make fairly confident assumptions as to the ideal channel and device types to best support the execution of their current task sets.

As we begin to examine more lengthy task sets, we can see that specific channels and devices are not always best equipped to cover the whole sequence. But given that we obviously cannot expect Janet to lurch back and forth between PC, phone and TV, for example, in the course of one task set (consider her activities above), we are obliged to consider that certain tasks may need to be shoehorned into channels and devices that are less than optimal, simply in order to provide the customer with the cohesive execution of the task set that she requires.

Thus it will increasingly be necessary for interface designers to accommodate small-screen mobile devices for tasks that may ideally require a larger display, in order to fit in with the usage patterns of customers.

TASK – THE ATOM OF VALUE AND TRUST
IN DIGITAL MARKETS

KEY POINT

If mode is the molecule of user expectation and experience, the task is the atom from which these encounters are built.

Customer modes – in particular the purposive elements of mode – determine variable families of tasks that need to be performed. Some may be automated by the system, others driven by direct interaction between the customer and the various interfaces presented by the environment.

Tasks – and the satisfactory support of their execution by customers – make up the currency of both meaning and trust in digital markets. It is a fundamental tenet of our argument in this book, that a careful analysis and ranking of the full range of related tasks in the context of a digital environment, leading through to the development of the appropriate range and hierarchy of partnerships to span the environment, forms the correct framework for the development of valued and valuable businesses in tomorrow's digital markets.

Types of task

In taking a structured approach to analysing tasks, it helps to draw some distinctions, and to remember the principle that customers undertake groups of tasks – what we call 'task sets', in pursuit of purposive activities.

Tasks of two major types can be distinguished, and we call these deliberate tasks and automated tasks.

Deliberate tasks

These are tasks that the customer undertakes in pursuit of intentional goals, and they are both initiated and completed by them. A further distinction between autonomous tasks and configuration tasks in digital markets needs to be drawn.

HE SAID ... SHE SAID ...

Jakob Nielsen's Alertbox, December 10, 2000:

WAP Field Study Findings

'... Very precise task analysis will be necessary for WAP services to succeed. Unfortunately, task analysis is a black art as far as most people are concerned and it is the least appreciated part of usability engineering. The traditional Web also suffers from poor task analysis, with many sites structured according to how company management thinks rather than how users typically approach their tasks.

'... Mobile services must target users with immediate, context-directed content. General services like shopping are less likely to succeed in the mobile environment. Indeed, in the list of services bookmarked by users, shopping hardly figures at all; sports and entertainment are the two big categories.

'Killing time is the perfect application for mobile devices because they are readily available when users are waiting around for something to happen. At the bus stop? Play a short game. In line for something? Read a paragraph of gossip. Stuck in traffic that doesn't move? Check the scores of your favourite teams.'

http://www.useit.com/alertbox/20001210.html

- *Autonomous tasks.* Autonomous tasks are performed consciously by customers through interaction via the range of touchpoints and channels supported by the environment and the businesses within it.

  Autonomous tasks make no permanent changes to the system, do not alter the customer's profile and demand no follow-through activity from the service, unless an e-mail reply or call-back is requested as a component of participation tasks. Registration with the system is not normally required in order to perform these tasks.

- *Configuration tasks*. These are tasks where the customer interacts with the system to personalise information or the interface, adjust the specifications that drive the performance of the
system, or transact.

  The impact of these tasks is to create changes within the system
  that will affect future interactions. They alter the customer's
  profile, or demand follow-through activity from one or more
  businesses in the system. Characteristically, such changes require registration with the system.

Automated tasks

Automated tasks will typically have been set up through some
initial *configuration* by or on behalf of the customer. They involve
scheduled or 'triggered' activities largely handled by the system,
where the triggers are normally various types of pre-agreed event.

Balancing deliberation with automation

Three aspects of the customer's purpose will determine the appropriate degree of automation vs. deliberation in the analysis of
task requirements. These are:

- the *complexity* of the decision-making process;
- the (outside) *expertise* needed by the customer as input to that
process; and
- the degree of emotional *concern* attached to the customer's
overall purpose.

Where the complexity of the tasks to be performed takes the form of
difficult calculation (as will typically be the case, for example, with
the purchasing and management of the more sophisticated financial instruments) the customer will expect the system to help out.

Where the complexity demands the application of specialised knowledge, the customer will be looking for not only
input from a trusted expert resource, but some degree of explana-

tion, if only for reassurance. It is likely that that customer will expect to participate actively in this process.

Where the degree of customer concern is high – as in the case of a matter of family health, a large financial outlay (or simply in an area of particular interest to the customer) – she will need to remain actively involved in the decision process and also informed of any key automated tasks that are about to be, or have been, performed.

Further determining factors are *perceived risk* and *reaction time*. These interact in the case of market sensitive tasks such as share dealing or bidding at auction, and the customer must have implicit trust in the service if she is to automate tasks where risk is endemic but delay may be more risky than not acting.

An example of balancing these tensions can be seen in the case of the automated tools that might be provided to assist the management of a share portfolio. Possible options for automation would be analysed in terms of urgency or speed of action required to limit risk, and the complexity of the customer's decision (Fig. 4.4).

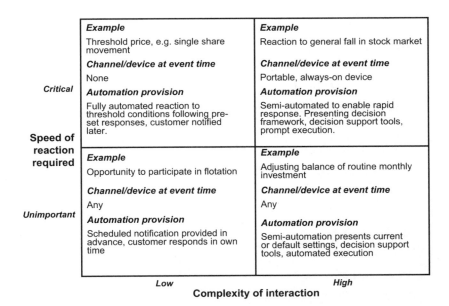

Fig. 4.4 Analysis of some of the options available for automating share-dealing services based on complexity and speed of response required to limit risk.

TASKS UNDER THE MICROSCOPE

Deliberate tasks

These are, as we have said, tasks that the customer undertakes in pursuit of intentional goals, and they are both initiated and completed by them. A further distinction between autonomous tasks and configuration tasks in digital markets needs to be drawn.

Autonomous tasks

Autonomous tasks are performed consciously by customers through interaction via the range of touchpoints and channels supported by the environment and the businesses within it.

They typically take four distinct forms:

- Exploration – which includes activities such as reading, browsing and viewing. Exploration is by definition a less-than-focused activity where the customer is, for part of the time, led by the information that she encounters.
- Analysis – the compilation, and in some instances comparison, of information, focused on the making of decisions, which would perhaps lead into the selection of products and/or services for purchase.
- Interaction – with human representatives of the business, with other members of communities or interest groups, and of course with friends, family and colleagues.
- Support – which includes inspection of trust credentials and consulting help services.

Configuration tasks

These are tasks where the customer interacts with the system to personalise information or the interface, adjust the specifications that drive the performance of the system, or transact.

Again, they typically take several forms:

- Formatting – which typically results in a change to the way that information, the interface or the activity sequence is configured for the customer.
- Transacting – involving ordering, paying for (where required) and arranging receipt of goods or services. Other transacting tasks include signing up for permission and request marketing materials and newsletters, or setting up and customising bespoke automated services.
- Posting – the permanent addition of information to public forums, discussion groups and shared services or to personal storage or records.

(Note that there can be subsequent customer tasks, as a consequence of transacting, such as taking receipt of physical goods, that take place outside the digital environment.)

Automated tasks
Automated tasks, as we have said, will typically have been set up through some initial configuration by or on behalf of the customer. They involve scheduled or 'triggered' activities largely handled by the system, where the triggers are normally various types of pre-agreed event.

Automated tasks fall into three categories:

- Scheduled – which are typically e-newsletters, reports and notifications or reminders that have been requested, or at least permitted, by the customer and are delivered on a regular basis by the system. These have simple triggers like time, or the availability of goods or services in which interest has been indicated.

Any response or follow-up is the responsibility of the customer.

- Co-effected – these are tasks completed largely by the system but which require decisions, approval or other interaction from the customer or their agents before final execution. The customer will have previously configured the type of response expected of the service when a particular threshold event occurs. The occurrence of the event provides the trigger and, in the case of co-effected tasks, will result in a direct communication with the customer, for example requesting some sort of refining input or approval.

- Independent tasks – these are fully-automated tasks that, though similarly triggered by threshold events, require no human interaction outside the system. The customer has instructed the system to execute in full, and may receive only a later notification that the task has been performed.

Note that over time an increasing number and range of conscious user-driven tasks will migrate downwards to become fully automated, independent tasks through the development of superior software, combined with a more profound understanding of how tasks and mode interact in digital markets.

THE PROGRESSIVE ENGAGEMENT CYCLE AND CUSTOMER LOYALTY

KEY POINT

It is through the apparently mundane process of task analysis that the stage is set for the most robust delivery of value, and eventually loyalty, in digital markets.

If customers' modes are met on each occasion with coherent task sets that are identified as relevant to their purposes, a cycle of interaction is set in motion that leads to progressively deeper engagement with the service.

Autonomous exploration that provides assurance that needs will be met, leads on to a purchase or other configuration activity that constitutes the first step of engagement.

Once trust is validated through a number of satisfactory outcomes to these initial, non-committal transactions, the stage is set for partial, and in time perhaps complete, transfer of some tasks to the system through automation. The customer has thus thoroughly integrated the service into her life – a new and very different model of loyalty (Fig. 4.5).

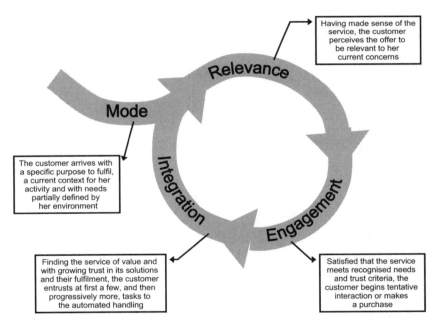

Fig. 4.5 The 'Cycle of Customer Engagement' leads from the discovery of relevance, through initial engagement to full integration, provided each stage meets with a satisfactory outcome.

AND BACK IN THE REAL WORLD ...

Tesco, the successful UK supermarket chain, has also become the world's most profitable Internet grocer. The company's development process for the service featured a high degree of customer task analysis.

One consequence of this was that Tesco made the unusual decision to integrate local stores fully into its on-line strategy, so that customers now make their on-line purchases from their most convenient location. This approach not only enabled the company to meet customers' needs more completely, but supported regional price variations which improved profits.

In terms of penetration, Tesco.com is heading for one million registered customers, with coverage of 90 percent of the UK, and weekly revenues of over £5m.

AN ASIDE

As an important aside, we need to register an apparently inescapable trend for the future. If the environment of digital markets is already becoming less than welcoming and chilly for the sentimental brand, *what happens when a constantly decreasing proportion of conscious participation between customer and brand in tomorrow's market space combines with increasing perceived inconvenience of such conscious interactions of the customer with the brand?*

Does brand in any meaningful sense at that point become entirely detached from value in digital markets: a mere sign over the door? Does the current plethora of channels and device types, after this recent explosion into the consciousness of the market and the customer, ultimately recede back down into the id of commercial life, while cyberlife becomes just a cultural blip in history?

TO SUMMARISE

- The promiscuous customer is unsentimentally focused on the work he or she wants to perform in the digital domain, and obstacles to that process immediately erode value and loyalty.
- The *paradox of mode* informs us that it is upon the most elementary and day-to-day customer tasks that we must first focus in developing our offer for digital markets.
- *Modal Analysis* – where the systematic consideration of customers' environmental, contextual and purposive needs provides a clear and value-focused account of where businesses may and may not usefully focus their efforts – is our proposed solution.
- The description and analysis of the customer *tasks* that unfold from their various *purposes* is the key output of Modal Analysis: tasks take a range of forms, under the overall headings of *deliberate* and *automated*.
- The satisfaction of customer mode through the support of key tasks sets up a cycle of engagement that leads the customer through an experience that will hopefully culminate in *integration*, where key tasks are assigned to the business; this is the foundation of future loyalty in digital markets.

CHAPTER 5

Meaning, Trust and Value

'... Now if you're ready, Oysters dear,
We can begin to feed.'
'But not on us!' the Oysters cried,
Turning a little blue.
'After such kindness, that would be
A dismal thing to do!'
'The night is fine,' the Walrus said.
'Do you admire the view?'

IN THIS CHAPTER WE LOOK AT

- some fundamental and common misconceptions about the role and value of *content*;
- how *meaning* is (re)created for information in digital markets by association with key customer task sets;
- the basics of *trust*, and our approach of Trustpoint Analysis;
- the close interplay between *meaning* and *trust* as customers interact with the system; and
- how the dual processes of the Cycle of Customer Need and the Cycle of Interaction link together, and how Modal Analysis enables the mapping of the delivery of value to the customer.

THE TWIN PILLARS OF VALUE IN DIGITAL MARKETS

We've seen in the previous chapters how the frustrations experienced by customers in digital markets frequently boil down to issues of meaning, trust, or a combination of the two. This chapter looks more closely at these misunderstood and underestimated imperatives, and prepares the ground for an introduction to 'marketspaces', the successful paradigm for creating value for both customers and businesses in tomorrow's digital markets.

This is as good a place as any to note the close linkage between meaning and trust in the customer experience … you simply can't have one without the other. An experience where trust is compromised immediately affects the customer's attainment of meaning, while of course a lack of meaning will – no surprise – cauterise for good any budding trust-building activity.

Let's now examine them more closely, starting with the combination of basic misconceptions and inherited thinking that has led the quest for meaning astray in the Commoditised Internet.

IT ALL SEEMED TO WORK OK BEFORE …

A bit of history

The major problems of meaning (as in the need to make sense of things) in traditional media have been solved long ago. There exist both established conventions, and also what can be called 'mutual assumptions', between producers and customers in, for example, film, TV and newspapers. Conventions in the sense that information as it relates respectively to specific areas of interest (sports, business, politics etc.) tends – and naturally this will vary between cultures – to be presented in a certain expected format, within a corresponding context. Assumptions that are mutual, in the sense that each side has predictable expectations about the behaviour of the other. Lengthy scene setting and explanatory clarification of terms is unnecessary and indeed counterproductive.

To give a brief example, a simple combinations of figures, such as '6–1' which, while out of context, can be altogether meaningless to the reader or at least open to a prohibitively wide range of interpretations, automatically becomes immediately and instinctively meaningful to the typical customer when in the context of a sports page, gambling odds, the stock markets or a basic maths problem. Notice here how the context is essential to meaning.

Not so fast …

In digital media – partly due to the general youth of the industry, partly due to the nature of the medium itself, and also to an extraordinary and ingrained tendency in the industry to treat abundance of information as synonymous with abundance of value – there exists as yet no such agreed protocol. Early attempts to introduce off-line material wholesale – i.e. with the context intact – into the digital environment, failed. Early Web sites developed for marketing purposes illustrate this well, importing brochure materials unmodified and assuming that the customer experience would echo that of the physical world.

At the time of writing therefore, each digital service – beyond at a basic level observing the grudgingly but increasingly accepted ground rules of usability – must try to support meaning in whatever contextual fashion it can, hampered further by the global reach of the medium. No *a priori* assumptions can safely be made about the customer's mode, preferences, culture – indeed anything at all – at the moment of arrival into the space.

Narrative, that other staple of meaning and learning, gets short shrift in digital media. By definition, in an interactive environment (despite all that glorious early talk about choosing the endings of your films!) narrative in digital media is cut off at its very root by the participation of the customer.

At a generic level, of course, the champions of usability have gone a long way towards pointing up some of the more absurd atrocities, but – with no disrespect at all intended to these noble folk – their work is closer in effect to that of the emergency room.

Now that the patient may live – at least for a while – let's see if we can help him make himself understood!

'BLAMESTORMING'

The double fantasy of the advertising model

The fantasy that, in digital markets, 'content is king' has been perpetrated by media owners, advertisers, and unsurprisingly, those businesses whose on-line revenue is advertising-driven, such as the search engines and directories.

Media owners have naturally been keen to find a role allowing them to leverage current and legacy material, with a view to generating additional streams of revenue. To this end they have re-launched it as *content* (a generic way of avoiding any tighter classification) and offered it on Web sites of all sorts, either through their own channels, by syndicating to portal owners, or in some cases both.

Yet, as we have pointed out elsewhere, content remains determinedly free and few businesses earn a direct return from customers willing to pay for it.

Despite this, to ensure that they could continue to ride the share accelerator that the technology bull market of 1999–2000 created, media owners subscribed to, and perhaps even had a hand in sustaining, the myth.

At its core lie two notions: that sheer volume of miscellaneous material is of value to customers and that, by providing it, media owners are key players in the 'new economy'. (The myth was embraced on the production and design side too, with the curious concept of 'stickiness'; the idea that 'compelling' content would of itself attract visitors, induce them to hang around longer and come back for more. Thus making them sitting ducks for a stream of – targeted of course – advertising messages. Thereby feeding the myth further.)

HE SAID ... SHE SAID ...

Jakob Nielsen's Alertbox, December 24, 2000

The Web in 2001: Paying Customers ... Beyond Advertising

'As I've said since 1997, advertising doesn't work on the Web because it is contrary to user behavior, which is largely goal-directed. Now, at the end of 2000, emerging trends are further validating my earlier analysis:

- Business plans don't get funded if they are based on advertising revenues.
- Web-based advertising agencies are downsizing.
- Click-through rates continue to drop and we continue to observe strong banner blindness in user testing. Users have stopped even clicking on useful page elements that *look* like ads.

'From 1997 through about mid-2000, it was possible to build Internet services using a business model based on separating gullible investors from their money. Because this is no longer feasible, the focus is now shifting to separating customers from their money. A much healthier way to build a business.'

http://www.useit.com/alertbox/20001224.html

The myth gathers momentum ...

This idea exactly complemented the need for advertising-supported Web sites to convince reluctant media buyers that there was real value in their audiences. So the myth became self-perpetuating, with portals – most of which originated as search engines, directories or related tools – convincing themselves their main objective was to keep customers hanging about their sites for as long as possible, and a majority of product marketers wanting a piece of the portal pie.

Adding fuel to the fire, many influential marketing agencies supported 'content is king' instinctively, perhaps because it's less work to assume that digital media is 'just another channel', subject to the same rules of engagement – and delivering the same outcomes – as the ones they are familiar with. The mantra also makes it sound reassuringly similar to the television and magazine markets, where aspirational selling to the passive and relatively indulgent entertainment and leisure audience is a well understood and indeed highly profitable art. (That it took years to work out how to use television for advertising is conveniently forgotten in the agencies' rush to prove to their clients that they are masters of this new medium too.)

For portals the approach made commercial sense (and who would argue, frankly, in that bull market) despite the risk of undermining the value of the original tools that brought customers in the first place. It did, after all, create enormous numbers of 'page impressions' that could be sold to would-be advertisers, and any awkward questions as to the value of an audience with this much time on their hands didn't arise until later.

AND BACK IN THE REAL WORLD ...

Interesting to note the comparison between two recent pieces of research at this point. Of the US $1234bn estimated as the total of Internet-generated revenue in the year 2002 by ActivMedia, Jupiter predicts a mere $6.8bn US will derive from on-line advertising.

ActivMedia quoted by Nua (www.nua.ie), Jupiter MMXI, 2001.

'Some publishers are already turning away from the Web. The *Wall Street Journal*'s WSJ Online, which got 60% of its revenue from advertising in 2000, saw ad revenues slip by 30% in the first 3 months of 2001. Dow Jones, its parent company, announced cutbacks to save $60m. Other media companies to slash their Web-based operations include the *New York Times* and News Corporation.'

'When Information is Worth Paying For', *Net Profit Europe*, May 2001.

And the upshot?

For product marketers, who after all were ultimately paying for this unholy three-way marriage, the result was a disaster. Customers had to be relentlessly entertained, 'lifestyle' impelled and generally 'relationship-managed' with material irrelevant to, and distracting from, the task in hand. Unwieldy animations and baroque decorative motives typically greeted their arrival, and thereafter they were often obliged to endure an ever-expanding selection of aspirational material in the name of a spurious assertion of community. Advertisers or sponsors were then sought – initially with great success – to help pay for this expensive nonsense.

Post-mortem notes on the king ...

Several things were fundamentally wrong here:

1   'Content is king' ignores, indeed abuses, the value of the customer's time.
2   Anything at all that deflects customers from the prompt fulfilment of their purpose, attacks trust and value and ultimately diminishes loyalty. The apparent exception to this rule in entertainment and games services immediately disappears when we examine the customer's purpose in visiting these sites. They come to be entertained, play games or kill time. (In these environments, stickiness works for the customer.)
3   Digital markets, with the possible exception of interactive television, do not easily lend themselves to aspirational selling. They are task-based channels created for the fulfilment of customers' purposes. These purposes may include identification with celebrities and staying abreast of fashion-driven markets as a form of entertainment, but rarely, for example, the impulse buying of luxury goods, whose lure and

cachet are diminished in this context. (It's no accident that would-be marketers of luxury goods were among the first to suffer in the shakeout following the change of market sentiment in the spring of 2000.)

4   Audiences who have the time and inclination to hang around absorbing this irrelevant material are, unsurprisingly, the ones that are least likely to make purchases. They are, in fact, the ones that a more rigorous marketing discipline would have qualified out of the sales process early on. Instead they are invited to hang out, slowing down the service for everyone else both structurally (all this extraneous, irrelevant content) and technically (overloading the servers). Supporting endless audience participation is not a free lunch. The problem extends to the audience offered to advertisers. Are they really as valuable as all that, if they are only ever window shoppers and not serious buyers?

But on the other hand ...

Contrary to the impression that might be created by the foregoing, information and therefore content is still a critical component of digital media. Information is what digital media handle best and, when it is intelligently applied to address customers' needs and fulfil their purpose, it enables the entire interaction. Without it, most contact is quite simply meaningless and most offers devoid of trust.

So what is the difference? Just this, information and relevant content used to support the customer's essential tasks, to validate solutions and enlarge understanding and opportunities is the servant of the user, capable of imparting meaning, growing trust and creating value. Disjointed content that screams for attention does the reverse, denying meaning, undermining trust and destroying value.

CORPORATE GATECRASHERS AT THE COMMUNITY BALL

A home of real value on the Internet

For the advocates of 'content is king', a further distorting mirror is introduced by the drive for 'community'. This critical component of user value was one of the earliest applications of the Internet, pre-dating the World Wide Web, and countless forums and discussion groups now exist, covering every kind of subject and concern.

Most communities, especially those on Usenet, are predicated on real communities of interest and fiercely reject commercialisation of their service. Some (such as those in the Parent Soup section of iVillage at the time of writing) do persist in a more commercial environment, and this co-existence is comfortable wherever real professional, medical, social or otherwise expert support can be exchanged, and where sensitivities and boundaries are carefully observed by entrants from business.

And it's true that in these cases content really is king, but not the content that media owners want to pedal. No, this content is entirely provided by users, trusted experts or mandated moderators. Thus (not least because in these environments customers are also producers) the 'mutual assumptions' we looked at earlier as lubricating meaning off-line, are actually very much present here, as are group-wide – and often fiercely enforced – protocols. This means that the potential for both meaning and trust in these authentic communities of interest is incomparably high.

Community and meaning

Community sites such as iVillage, which are services dedicated to information, collaboration and support for social groupings or communities of interest who share common concerns, assign a healthy degree of meaning to digital environments. This arises from two primary characteristics. First, depending on the breadth of focus of the service and the degree to which its users therefore share interests in common, a certain degree of prior understanding and known 'context' can be assumed. Secondly, the users create much of the content themselves, in discussion groups and forums and through posted reviews and messages; this creates a sense of shared ownership and values.

Having said that, many of the well-known community services are fundamentally publishing ventures and suffer from some of the vices we have been examining: an obsession with volume, lack of clarity about boundaries and a reliance on advertising revenue, with all that that entails.

THE NEW ROAD TO MEANING

KEY POINT

It's becoming very clear: unlike traditional media, the medium in digital markets intrinsically assigns little or no contextual or convention-based meaning to information. In fact, the nature of the medium tends to strip meaning away, leaving information raw and out of context.

The information itself, hacked by necessity into ever-smaller pieces, can no longer take its context with it. This creates work for the customer in establishing a sufficient degree of relevance.

What's the answer? You've already got it, actually. Meaning is brought back to the orphaned information in digital markets by its attachment to the tasks customers need to perform. Meaning here is no longer a fixed attribute of information, it's now a potential attribute whose missing chemical is the current purpose of the promiscuous customer.

Only Modal Analysis, where the information is assessed, shaped and hung on a framework created from the potential purposes and task sets of customers, can bring content, context and customer together to create value.

AND BACK IN THE REAL WORLD …

W. W. Grainger, the huge US business-to-business supplier of maintenance products and spare parts, has invested heavily in integrating off- and on-line services to help customers make sense of its catalogue of over 250,000 individual products. While the company's enormous range has been doubled with the launch of its Web offering, and the site's navigation and search functions are carefully thought through, it still encourages customers to simplify their choices by consulting with its well-trained branch personnel.

A CLOSER LOOK AT HOW TRUST WORKS

Generic trust issues

There are of course two generic trust issues without which any digital service cannot realistically trade. They are more than adequately covered elsewhere, and we mention them here only in order to be able to move forward to more pertinent pastures. Clearly, security of transactions and credit, and security and privacy of customer data, are must-haves in any digital trading environment.

It is worth noting in passing, however, that customers' overall impression of the adequacy of these essentials is more often influenced by basic usability concerns than by other, perhaps more technical, issues. In other words, a smooth and task-supportive experience does more to support this aspect of trust than shrill protestation or third-party verification.

The critical role played by trust in digital markets

While the customer's preoccupation – conscious or otherwise – with trust revolves essentially around the minimising of perceived risk through reassurance, we distinguish a number of examples of

KEY POINT

Above all else, trust plays the following absolutely critical role in any digital market. It is the vehicle that moves a customer from the essential but transitional stage of 'generally positive brand experience and perception', across the divide of doubt, to taking action, to making a firm commitment, typically, but not invariably, in the form of a purchase. Trust, in other words, sorts the commercial wheat from chaff, sheep from goats.

roles played by trust in the customer experience. Trust is, as we can see, in many respects a chameleon entity, contributing to navigation, risk reduction, decision enabling, generic reassurance, relationship building and so on.

The concept of 'trustpoints'

So, how to deal effectively with this critical concern? We use an approach called 'Trustpoint Analysis'.

Customers' trust requirements evolve over time. Initial reassurance, fol-

---

HE SAID ... SHE SAID ...

'To gain the loyalty of customers, you must first gain their trust. That's always been the case, but on the Web, where business is conducted at a distance, and risks and uncertainties are magnified, it's truer than ever. On-line, customers can't look a sales clerk in the eye, can't size up the physical space of a store or office, and can't see and touch products. They have to rely upon images and promises, and if they don't trust the company presenting those images and promises, they'll shop elsewhere. In fact, when we asked Web shoppers to name the attributes of e-tailers that were most important in earning their business, the number one answer was "a Web site I know and trust". All other attributes, including lowest cost and broadest selection, lagged far behind. Price does not rule the Web; trust does.'

'E-loyalty: Your Secret Weapon on the Web', *Harvard Business Review*, July/August 2000.

lowed by consistent performance, paves the way for trustpoint support to provide reassurance and introduce pledges that reduce barriers to customer progression. The reassurance required therefore changes as experience develops.

At each stage in this cycle customers will have different needs:
- for task support;
- for reassurance;
- for information and usage support; and
- to minimise complexity.

These concerns need to be met with clear, optional provision and are not successfully addressed by complicating the access process and putting 'must view' barriers in the customers' path.

My loyalty to Amazon and Avant-Go (for example) is fostered not by brand communications, but by an ongoing incremental increase in value which is delivered at key trustpoints.

Equally, when only the less valuable customer types tend to be receptive to pushed marketing messages (just as the lonely consumer on whom outbound telephone campaigns depend is big on time and short on company), how much resource can be reasonably expended here?

Trustpoints occur ever more frequently in contact cycles in digital markets, as communications and transactions occur both faster and more often. This is also happening because customers are increasingly in direct digital contact with suppliers: the

KEY POINT

Trustpoints are those typically small yet critical events in the customer contact cycle, where trust (in this case an 'inclination to commit') is either grown or eroded. It is impossible to overestimate their importance in digital markets. They offer to the business the chance (indeed the inevitable duty) to exercise the appropriate trust drivers in answer to the customer's question.

Trustpoints exist independently of brand communications, and while the customer's brand loyalty can certainly be massaged upwards by non-interruptive and non-dissonant communications, woe betide the company whose claims are not met or ideally exceeded in the digital marketplace.

AND BACK IN THE REAL WORLD ...

'Another exemplary company that uses trust as the foundation for loyalty is the Vanguard Group. The fastest-growing mutual fund company over the past decade, with more than $500 billion in assets currently under management, Vanguard has poured over $100 million into the development of its Web site. Unlike many of its competitors, Vanguard doesn't use the site to hype its products. Rather, it uses its on-line presence to inform and educate its customers – even when that means leading them *away* from a purchase. When you click through Vanguard's pages, you are often warned against investing in certain funds ...

'... eBay used the unique capabilities of the Web to establish and enforce rules of engagement. Buyers and sellers rate each other after every transaction, and the ratings are posted on the site; every member's reputation thus becomes public record.'

'E-loyalty: Your Secret Weapon on the Web', *Harvard Business Review*, July–August 2000.

corresponding decline in the number of intermediated experience tends to create a more "raw" encounter that is unbuffered.

In other words, risk – perceived or real – is heightened, and the user can also feel isolated and in a more defensive stance.

THE BASICS OF TRUSTPOINT ANALYSIS

'The 10 Rs' – key trust drivers in digital markets

When a customer's contact cycle with a business leads her to a trustpoint, a question is asked of the business, a question that's loaded in the sense that a correct or relevant response automatically grows trust, while the opposite either erodes or destroys it.

So we must turn to the customer's contact cycle with the business, to identify, analyse and manage those behaviours which support and build customer trust (see Fig. 5.1).

These, we believe, are the ten *sine qua non*s for building trust in digital markets. (Note that, while perhaps irritatingly they all begin with 'R', relationship does not appear here!)

In approximate order of encounter:

1   *Reputation.* (Company X are 'nice people to do business with' and carry appropriate endorsements. They seem to be stand-up citizens and they keep good company in their alliances and suppliers.)

2   *Reassurance.* (Company X are proactively clear with me about issues that concern me, and treat my concerns seriously.)

3   *Respect.* (Company X don't bombard me with inappropriate marketing messages or offers – they speak when they're spoken to.)

4   *Response.* (Company X act and react quickly and decisively, from the initial interface right through to delivery.)

5   *Responsibility.* (Company X look after my needs right through the process.)

6   *Recognition.* (Company X use my information to help me get what I want, not to make me do what they want.)

7   *Reliability.* (The service of Company X worked for me last time, it works today, it'll work even better tomorrow.)

8   *Reward.* (Company X reward loyalty, patience, hanging in there with service problems etc.)

9   *Rest.* (Company X know when to give it a rest!)

10 *Repetition.* (Now do it again! But better …)

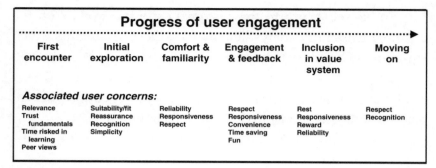

Fig. 5.1 Evolving trust requirements as user engagement changes. (Note that the need for these elements of trust support of course varies, according to the customer's familiarity with the environment.)

HOW MEANING AND TRUST PLAY OUT
IN DIGITAL MARKETS

Upon first entering a digital space, a customer's first requirement is generally to find answers to two simple questions: 'So what?' and 'OK, what's in it for me?' We've already looked closely at customer mode, and it's mode that determines just how these questions are asked, and therefore need to be answered.

To understand the sequence, we need to examine how the various influences interact. The customer encounter progresses through identifiable stages of need for:

- the discovery of meaning;
- the building of trust;
- the experience of value; and
- the formation of commitment, which is independently reinforced as tasks are assigned to automation.

These do not supersede each other, rather they co-exist throughout the cycle, each building on the foundation laid by its predecessors. Figure 5.2 captures these progressive stages, in the same way that we previously showed the Cycle of Engagement for mode, relevance, engagement and integration.

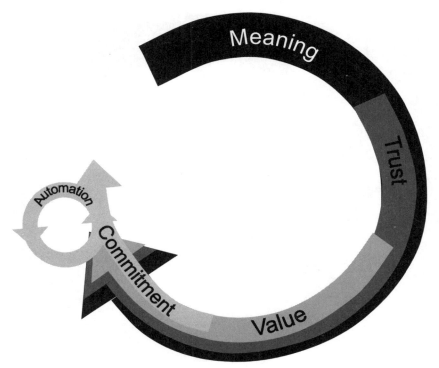

Fig. 5.2 The Cycle of Perception, commencing from meaning and trust and leading to the discovery of value and finally to commitment. Note that theoretically over time the automation cycle at the left will enlarge, as the customer commits to a greater number of automated services.

The 'Cycles of Customer Experience' tool

The two cycles of engagement and perception connect throughout the process, constantly feeding each other (Fig. 5.3).

1 Starting with the Cycle of Engagement (the inner cycle which describes the customer's direct encounter with the space):

2 As *mode* is – we hope – met with an adequate degree of *relevance* ...

3 ... the experience begins to increase the degree of *meaning* achieved in the mind of the customer ...

4 ... which in turn triggers the beginning of *trust*.

5 As *relevance* 'crystallises', and becomes accepted ...

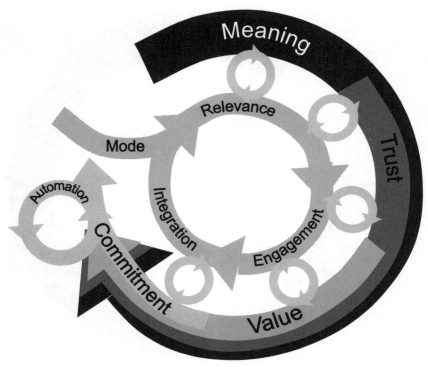

Fig. 5.3 The complete Cycles of Customer Experience (the inner Cycle of Engagement and the outer Cycle of Perception) and their dynamic relationship in building meaning, trust, value and ultimately commitment in the customer.

6   … the encounter moves ahead on the cycle …

7   … to enable the start of *engagement* as the customer begins to use the service to execute her tasks.

Satisfactory engagement and reinforced trust together pave the way for the delivery of value. (Note that this analysis is equally applicable to the overall customer contact cycle and to a unique customer session in the space.)

Most interestingly, given our earlier questioning of CRM, it is at this point (and not a moment before) that the customer's experience of value encourages her to consider assigning certain tasks and/or task sets to the space, as automated functions. At this integration stage, she configures the desired services, setting thresholds and other personal requirements, thereby establishing the basis for the paradoxical 'unconscious loyalty' we look at below. We call this the stage of commitment, and its self-reinforcing character is the Holy Grail of successful players in future digital markets. But we can never sit back on our laurels: each new mode that our customer brings to the service needs to be met with the same, careful escalating cycle.

MEANING AND TRUST REVISITED – HOW IT SHOULD BE ...

A better banking experience for Christopher

You'll remember Christopher's brand-eroding experience with his bank's Internet service, WebWonga, how it directly attacked his support for, and loyalty to, the bank's brand through its failure to observe the importance of meaning and trust.

How would a positive experience in WebWonga shape up in contrast, where the imperatives of meaning and trust are supported by the adoption of Modal Analysis?

Using our merged Cycles of Customer Experience, we can walk with him through a different experience that, through the bank's recognition of the need for support of meaning and trust, not only satisfies his primary purpose, but sets the scene for an improved service to Christopher, and (while we're, as you will have gathered, suspicious of the term 'loyalty') goes some way towards strengthening the relationship too. So, referring closely to Fig. 5.3:

Christopher's mode upon approaching what we'll call the WebWonga 'space' (we're keen at this point to begin to extend our thinking beyond Web sites) for the first time in earnest after his change from the PC-based service, can be described under our three subheadings of *mode*.

His *purpose* is, for the sake of this example, to pay some bills online. Note that he may, having entered the space, develop one or more secondary or indeed unrelated purposes, but at this point we are describing his *primary* purpose, which as you'd imagine determines whether or not the space delivers any kind of immediate satisfaction.

His *environment* is at home working on his laptop through a dial-up account (although note that he will be seeking eventually to perform some of these types of task through his PDA).

His *context* is that he has made the decision to solve an 'off-line' problem – that of paying some bills – using a digital facility. Note that he's also a new user of the service.

For the initial stage of Christopher's contact to be adequate, therefore, he needs an environment that supports relatively low bandwidth (but equally is not totally stripped down), that offers both generic and more task-specific learning and FAQs (without necessarily forcing him to jump through these hoops – remember that he's a confident Web user), and that is able to recognise early in the session that his purpose is that of seeking to pay bills.

A clear and early 'recognition' by the system of Christopher's primary purpose, that is demonstrated by the provision of support for the entire task set derived from that purpose (using one device across the whole set) and that also reflects his status as a new user, contributes hugely to the provision of an early experience of 'relevance'; that in turn enables Christopher to rapidly make sense of the environment in terms of his purpose.

In other words, this early experience with WebWonga has enabled a high degree of *meaning*. Note also that there has been no promotional aspect to the experience so far, no extraneous advertising (targeted or otherwise) or product offers.

The enabling of meaning therefore builds into the enabling of an embryonic trust.

Christopher can now proceed with confidence to perform the task set which his purpose has determined, and because the bank has done its Modal Analysis work in a diligent fashion, he's able to complete the payment of three bills with ease.

And here's where the notion of 'stickiness' makes a brief re-appearance in a far more acceptable form. Having built a mini-platform of meaning and trust, and having also engaged with the service by executing a coherent purpose, Christopher will (either during this session or a future one, or indeed both) be far more disposed to explore the WebWonga space for other services that may be of interest to him.

In other words, he is moving into the stage we call (and check back with the Cycles diagram here if you need to) 'engagement', and his experience is now creating real value for him.

In the course of the satisfactory performance of the task set involved in paying his bills, and later in his less focused exploration of the WebWonga space, Christopher will have been offered the opportunity to have the bank automate some or all of the tasks he's been performing deliberately. To take a simple and familiar example he can, with some simple configuration work, set up direct debits for two out of the three utility bills he's just paid.

So the meeting of Christopher's needs in terms of meaning, trust and value, using the technique of Modal Analysis, sets the scene for the Holy Grail of customer relationships in digital markets.

By assigning – at what we call the stage of integration – certain key tasks to the bank (and of course this is likely to increase further as time passes, assuming a generally satisfactory contact cycle with WebWonga), he is establishing – and note that it's the customer who does this, not the business – a commitment to the relationship with the bank that goes far deeper than what can be achieved with any CRM program. This, if you like, is Customer-Managed Relationship (or C-MR).

Take a second here and reflect that this powerful endgame has been made possible only through the approach of Modal Analysis.

'Unconscious customer loyalty' in digital markets

A paradox that we have uncovered during the process of writing this book is that, while a central element of brand loyalty in traditional marketing is considered to be share of mind (for example, a customer's consciousness of the brand at the key moment of commitment to purchase), in digital markets the communications that typically derive from the old-marketing approach are interruptive and lacking in relevance, therefore brand-erosive.

Extraordinarily, at first sight, loyalty in digital markets is crystallised when the customer moves around the cycle (see Fig. 5.3 above) from the satisfactory experience of engagement to the critical decision to integrate one or more of a space's automation services. This critical stage being discernible when, for example, the customer assigns a series of key tasks to the system, and sets the various thresholds required for the system to perform these tasks on his behalf.

The progressive nature of the engagement bears emphasis. Only after one or more experiences of 'having been recognised' by the marketspace, of having had his specific current mode met with meaningful relevance, and from there having been enabled to comprehensively execute the task set that derived from that mode, are the customer's experiences of both value and trust sufficiently high to support the assignment of work that can be automated in the future.

How interesting and how paradoxical that, with both value and trust being arguably higher than ever before in digital markets, the ultimate expression of loyalty is to consign – almost to dismiss – key interactions to the unconscious mind of the machine. This is the very opposite of mindshare, yet surely far more powerful.

TO SUMMARISE

- While off-line conventions as applied to traditional media support a reasonably high degree of *meaning*, these protocols have yet to be established in digital markets, placing the onus on customers to work harder.
- The commonly-held notion 'content is king' has brought about extraordinary and far-reaching strategic errors in the development of digital channels.
- This fantasy has been carried forward with vigour by media owners, advertisers and advertising-driven businesses.
- This in turn has caused marketers to entirely lose focus on real customer needs, and equally depleted the value of digital services to customers, by withholding support for the execution of tasks in the interest of delivering brand exposure to advertisers.
- This disaster can be repaired only through a rigorous focus on customer mode, where information is attached to purposes and tasks to achieve maximum relevance and support.
- The issue of *trust* in digital markets is huge, and closely intertwined with that of *meaning*: going beyond the traditional trust concerns, we must examine the entire customer contact cycle with the business – using the approach we call Trustpoint Analysis – to ensure that customer needs are anticipated and met at each stage.
- The true nature of the customer's cycle of encounters with the digital business shows how Modal Analysis enables the delivery of *value*, and supports the potential for a new kind of loyalty. This loyalty is expressed when the customer assigns certain key tasks to the business for automated performance on his or her behalf.

- This produces the paradox of 'unconscious customer loyalty', where the brands to which the customer is most loyal will tend over time to be those with which he or she has a diminishing range and number of encounters.

CHAPTER 6

Taking Stock

'That's the most important piece of evidence we've heard yet,' said the King, rubbing his hands; 'so now let the jury – '

'If any one of them can explain it,' said Alice, (she had grown so large in the last few minutes that she wasn't a bit afraid of interrupting him) 'I'll give him sixpence. I don't believe there's an atom of meaning in it.'

A SUMMARY OF THE DISCUSSION TO DATE

At this point we pause and review our conclusions. In the first five chapters we have contended the following:

Customers are a problem ...

- Customers have come to expect unprecedented levels of service in digital markets as a substitute for human contact: they have become fickle, promiscuous customers.
- The current lack of any convincing support for the creation of meaning in most digital services, and the consequent onus on

the customer to do much of the work, destroys trust and with it loyalty.

- CRM is no substitute: it can reinforce loyalty, but it cannot create it.

Brands are also a problem ...

- Neither can traditional branding compensate in the digital environment: the encounter is too immediate and too unmediated for any adequate form of meaning to be conveyed under the banner of simple identity, or through lifestyle association.
- In this environment, the brand is experienced primarily through the mechanics of the interaction and, as it is created and recreated in the experience of each contact, the customer in a very real sense 'owns' it and judges it.
- Furthermore, the limitless ways in which the brand can be encountered by customers in, for example, the multitude of search and reference sites, are largely out of the owner's control.

There are few sustainable business and revenue models ...

- If the interaction between customer and brand in the current digital environment is unsatisfactory, the constraints for companies doing business are often worse.
- The transparency of the market, coupled with the prevailing focus on business efficiency, has led to a transaction cost driven model of the value added, increasingly focusing the customer on price, and often price alone.
- This focus commoditises everything on offer, stripping value from differentiated products, and ensuring that, for most vendors, scale, reach and operational efficiency are the only available strategic levers.

- Despite some remarkable success stories among focused niche providers, most of the new 'business models' bear witness to these fundamentals ...
- ... and, in the end, value is not added for customers: far from it, the separate silos of information and islets of relevant product, constantly frustrate their larger purpose. Value is in fact diminished.

A new world of customer purpose

- The problem arises in part from a core misunderstanding of customer expectations and experiences in digital markets. Such markets are not like supermarket shelves where products compete to attract attention and advertise their virtues: they are, with the exception of entertainment, intensely demanding and dry, task-focused environments.
- In this impersonal interaction, anything that stands between the customer and the achievement of her purpose creates a dissonant experience that quickly undermines the perception of relevance and destroys trust. Marketing messages in this context are rarely welcome suggestions, more often destructive intrusions.
- Customers' real needs and expectations are driven by their overall purpose, as well as by their current activity and environment at the time of the encounter.

The critical benefits brought by Modal Analysis

- We have defined this context-dependent information as the customer's *mode*. To better serve our customers in digital markets, we need to understand all their various modes of interaction and the task sets that they give rise to, in order to service their full value chain.

- Equally critical for the understanding of mode, is the context created for the service and for the fostering of trust.
- Without a suitable contextual framework, the customer has to work hard to interpret the content, and to contrive meaning and trust. A high volume of information that is unrelated to the task set, is just as effective in destroying relevance as 'off-mode' communication.
- Trust is realised through a much more complex web of experiences than are embodied in the now-familiar concerns regarding security and privacy. Important as these are, it is through the support, validation, choice and respect that the service provides, in the minutiae of the experience throughout the interaction, that lasting trust is built.
- When a customer's mode of interaction is fully and consistently met with relevant information and support, a progressive cycle of engagement is triggered whose success is complete when she becomes willing to entrust elements of the task set to the system for automated handling. The outcome is not so much loyalty (displayed through conscious choice) as integration into the customer's life (manifest in unconscious trust).
- In summary, the customer must be supported through her cycle of need from discovery of meaning and establishment of trust, through the realisation of value, and into the final phase of commitment.

AND THE CONSEQUENCES FOR BUSINESS?

The implications of customer purpose

- For organisations seeking to utilise digital markets for purposes other than providing a no-frills source for entertainment or commoditised goods and services, the complexity of the customer interaction and the requirement to support meaning and trust raise questions about the appropriate form and structure of the service organisation.

- Significant conclusions to be drawn from the above analysis include:

  1 Most interactions are part of a substantial chain of activities that will be required to fulfil a single customer purpose. Simply servicing a small step in any of these chains creates fragmentation, entailing work for the customer and increasing frustration.

  2 Satisfactory experiences arise when each step of the customer's exploration is met with relevant information and advice that don't require additional work to locate and validate.

  3 Long-term value and regular use depend on the perception that a whole range of task sets, that meet conceivable purposes within a coherent domain of concern, are met by the service.

  4 Over time, customers will migrate to services that provide the greatest coverage of those domains of concern of most relevance to them, and that simplify the handling of essential tasks.

  5 Once a potential product or service that meets some component of the customer's need has been identified, several further consequences arise if trust is to be preserved;

    - *Neutrality*: a full range of the relevant and available products or services must be provided, not merely a single proprietary brand.
    - *Support*: the customer must have access to and assistance with all likely configurations.
    - *Trust services*: trustworthy, independent recommendation and validation must be available.
    - *Community*: communication and collaboration with others sharing the same concern must be supported.
    - *Service*: the experience of order fulfilment, delivery, installation and ongoing service must be satisfactory.

- *Flexibility*: responsiveness to the customer's varying modes of engagement.
- *Extension*: recognition that the customer's concerns do not cease to be important, and have consequences when they are not actively engaged with the service or using a purchased product.

So what needs to change?

- An extended service model is implied, one that caters for the whole range of relevant customer concerns, and within which external contributors of expertise and validation provide critical components.
- Effective digital markets that embrace real customer concerns, are in effect platforms for services. Product sales are essentially incidental to satisfying larger purposes, and the decreasing margins in product sales make adequate profitability from this source alone unlikely.
- To exploit this phenomenon effectively, companies will need to learn to devise and support reliable service offerings that customers are willing to pay for.
- The more these services enable the reduction of work for the customer through automation, the more commitment is fostered and the loyalty objective of companies is met.

AND THE IMPACT ON COMPANIES WHO WISH TO PARTICIPATE?

- These outcomes are more congenial for some organisations than others.
- They tend to conflict with the revenue and profit maximisation objectives of commodity product and service companies because:

- the additional costs of expertise, validation and services tend to increase the cost of sales;
- they imply (anathema to marketers) equal provision of attention to competitive products;
- and (anathema to salesmen) a need to invite third parties to arbitrate in a final buying decision.
- Others however, especially companies whose information, knowledge and expertise support relevance and meaning, and who may form the foundation for appropriate services, will find the new environment more congenial.
- Essentially, core strategies need to focus not on a targeted market segment, so much as on the key drivers of customer concern, accepting that those concerns generate purposive behaviour, that is common to a broad collective that cuts across market segments.
- Enterprises need therefore to provide the means to encourage the progressive maturation of the relationship into unconscious commitment, rather than relying on attempts to massage loyalty through insistent marketing communications.

INTRODUCING THE MARKETSPACE

- In the coming chapters, we explore what we call the *marketspace*, a configuration of components that fully satisfies customer modes of interaction in most potential digital markets, by providing a platform that meets the needs for:
  - the provision of relevant and credible information integrated into the service;
  - ready availability of independent expert advice and learning;
  - external support of trust in the form of various authoritative validating services (a form of third-party certification) ...

- ... and internal support of trust in the form of completeness of the offer and the backup of expert or user reviews;
- (increasingly) for ways to communicate and collaborate with other customers and interested parties; and
- simplification of the customer task set through automation of repetitive and critical tasks.

KEY POINT

The essential characteristics of a marketspace mean that the value lies in the context of use, and is enhanced by accessibility and familiarity. The dimensions of competition now change, and the core driver is the provision of support for purposive activity rather than minimisation of transaction costs.

- Critically, marketspaces provide a paradigm for independent product or service providers to co-operate with sources of information, expertise and validation.
- They are marked by their comprehensive nature – meeting all reasonable needs across the set – and their clear 'remit'. As we shall see, while a certain amount of flexibility in the boundaries of a marketspace is essential, it cannot expand far beyond its recognised bounds without losing definition and meaning.
- Having explored the characteristics of marketspaces and some of the trends that are fostering their creation, we will turn our attention to the implications for participating businesses. Chapters 8 and 9 explore the roles that marketspaces require, some of the benefits that different businesses might obtain, and the various implications for relationships and business strategy.
- Finally we will be looking at some current and future trends in an attempt to divine the future locus of real value for the customer, and therefore for the business, and the prospects for adoption of workable models for digital markets.

CHAPTER 7

The Marketspace – a New Paradigm for Value

'Now, if you'll only attend, Kitty, and not talk so much, I'll tell you all my ideas about Looking-glass House. First there's the room you can see through the glass – that's just the same as our drawing room, only the things go the other way.'

IN THIS CHAPTER WE LOOK AT

- the key generic components of marketspaces;
- the critically different customer experience in marketspaces, with a detailed worked example;
- how Modal Analysis and marketspaces will connect and work together;
- how marketspaces will thereby solve the three problems of 'silo syndrome'; and
- a broad summary of the benefits to key business types that will be conferred by this new paradigm.

THE MARKETSPACE CONCEPT

We've recognised that the Commoditised Internet contains little of value for either businesses or their customers, and is therefore unsustainable for most purposes and needs to evolve into a new value-based model.

It is, we contend, only by offering task-based meaning, trust and thereby ultimately value, that businesses in digital markets will achieve anything approaching the kind of success and loyalty they seek in this highly critical and emotionally neutral environment.

We've concluded that the successful trading model in digital markets will need to accommodate a range of information, expertise and validation components, that it must provide additional support for trust by offering a complete range of products, and that an extensive range of services is essential. And we have suggested that successful models might take the shape of what we are calling 'marketspaces'. These will in essence be highly flexible, truly customer-focused vehicles for positioning the various types of participating businesses optimally to deliver, and therefore reap the most value from, the task sets that the customer needs to execute in digital markets, derived from their current purpose, and expressed in their current mode.

Marketspaces will share many common features and similar components. They will be differentiated through their vision and focus, and the way in which they deploy their components in pursuit of value.

Building on the additional components that we loosely identified in the summary that concluded Chapter 5 as required to support the customer task set and foster meaning and trust, we can identify the major generic elements that will typically play roles in all marketspaces.

Figure 7.1 captures these generic components.

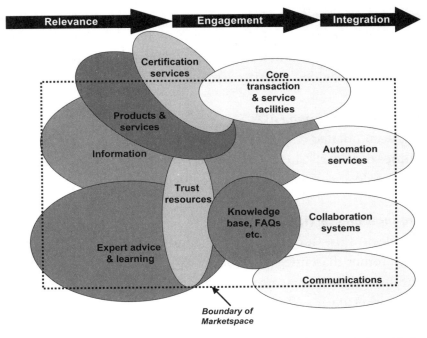

Fig. 7.1 The generic components of marketspaces, (showing their correlation with the steps of the Cycle of Engagement).

Identifying marketspace components

The following descriptions identify and distinguish the separate elements and indicate their contribution.

Information

The directories, reports, research, statistics, data, product and service listings, news, features and archive components that provide the raw material to inform structured tasks or queries.

Certification services

Externally validated certification and other authentication services, including public keys, credit ratings and guarantees, insurance, review and rating services. They are the external guarantors of trust for the service.

Expert advice and learning

A generic name for the market-specific advice, structured learning, expert systems and internal and external consultation services that are provided to help customers.

Knowledge base and FAQs

The accumulated responses of the company and customers to enquiries of all sorts and the discussion threads generated, collected to provide a searchable resource for all users.

Products and services

A collective title for products of all kinds, financial and other services (other than integral components of marketspace facilities) and subscriptions that are relevant to and made available through the marketspace.

Trust resources

The trustpoint support provided by the market owner, ranging from security and encryption, through personal data access and revision, to step-by-step guidance and support for identified trust components of the task set, or to validation of information and knowledge.

Core transaction and service facilities

Marketspaces must support a full range of configurable transaction and account management facilities, which may also include:

- bid and offer systems;
- auctions;
- requests for tender;
- demand aggregation applications;
- request for quotation facilities;
- enablement of purchase on or through appropriate exchanges;

- hedging and other risk-reduction facilities;
- purchase finance;
- management of accounts within the marketspace, especially those based on subscriptions or small incremental payments used to support automated services; and
- support for micropayments (sums smaller than a credit card can be used for).

Search engines, appropriate financial analysis tools, and a range of fulfilment services are also required.

Automation services

The core additional value-adding components of the marketspace lie in automation, embodied in three service types (all configured by customers, and where appropriate, built in response to customer needs):

- Simple, mass-customised digital services such as e-mail newsletters, product release notifications etc.
- Enhanced customer facilities including a wide range of individual organisational tools (diary, filing and storage facilities, account aggregation), more complex ASP services and expert systems for decision support and personal business management. These are included under automation services because automated notification, management and synchronisation facilities greatly enhance their value to customers.
- Automated services ranging from fully automated facilities independently executing commands dependent on trigger conditions, to partially automated services requiring user intervention or approval.

Collaboration systems

Peer-to-peer and distributed computing features shareable among market members, the trust resources needed to warrant them and any required transaction enablers. This may include synchronous file sharing, conferencing and collaborative document and picture creation tools, as well as asynchronous direct search and discovery tools, discussion groups, notification and reminder services and shared transaction facilities. Trust resources may include moderators, automatic screening and user ratings.

Communication systems

Voice (and video) conferencing, instant messaging, chat rooms, e-mail conferences and so on.

As suggested above, the significance and configuration of these facilities will depend on the industry domain in which the marketspace functions and on its focus, its vision and the specifics of its differentiation from other similar services.

HOW MARKETSPACES WILL PLAY OUT FOR CUSTOMERS

The Commoditised Internet revisited

We noted a range of frustrations experienced by customers in digital markets in Chapter 3, 'What's Wrong with the Internet?'.

While the majority of these emerged as in one or more ways compromising to meaning and trust, and while we have recognised that Modal Analysis can pre-empt many such problems, we can now review how marketspaces with the full range of facilities will be able, as a paradigm for successful future digital business, to break through these challenges to create real and repeatable value for customer.

We talked about the digital customer (outside the entertainment model) as being primarily focused upon solving problems. In this setting, the accommodation – above all else – of the customer's current purpose within the overall area of interest, and the task sets that derive from that purpose, are the central determinants of the attainment of meaning, trust, value and, perhaps over time, commitment.

How then will marketspaces deliver, where the Commoditised Internet so visibly fails?

A WORKED MARKETSPACE EXAMPLE: 'GOKIDS'

The 'GoKids' marketspace

GoKids is a marketspace in the childcare field, created to serve both the end consumer (typically parents) and business users such as childcare professionals and teachers. Here we unpack this sample marketspace to examine all of its key elements and dynamics.

Typical customer types

Let's work with our two customer types, Christopher and Janet; we'll reintroduce them briefly. Christopher you may recall is a designer, and the divorced parent of a 13 year-old son. Janet is also a parent and teaches science in a large public school.

Christopher's concerns and purposive activities

Christopher will typically come to GoKids for assistance with the following parental concerns for his child:

- health (both prevention and cure) and safety;
- development (physical, mental and spiritual); and
- 'best practice' in parenthood.

He will enter the GoKids Marketspace with these types of purposive activity in mind:

- to source reliable and trustworthy, expert, child-specific advice;

- to get rapid and clear solutions for ad hoc 'emergency' issues ...
- ... including 'Finding the Right Trusted Local Resource';
- to get assistance with product and service specification;
- to configure and purchase various products and services;
- to configure and use various news and offers services, including personal concerns such as food allergies;
- to contribute to – and get information from – various trusted 'community recommendation' services (especially nannies, schools, other sensitive concerns);
- to contribute to – and get information from – a 'community concerns' forum (emotional problems, abuse, addictions etc.);
- to access a parent support helpline;
- to hold dialogues with experts of various kinds; and
- to set up a diary of school-related events that will provide automated reminders of his obligations.

Janet's concerns and purposive activities

Janet's concerns will in many instances mirror those of Christopher, but there will also be some professional issues that are particular to her business, such as risk support and professional 'best practice'.

In her professional capacity she may also enter the GoKids marketspace with these types of purposive activity in mind:

- to gain access to CPD and e-learning support;
- to participate in – and get support from – industry lobbying groups;
- to participate in – and get support from – special issue-based groups;
- perhaps to utilise a recruitment service to contact potential staff; and

- to locate teaching aids and materials or configure automatic notifications.

Some generic examples of purposive activity that Christopher or Janet may wish to carry out
From the above, brief analysis we can derive some generic purposive activities that the marketspace must support:

- Get 'official' advice (e.g. from qualified experts). Typical task sets might include:
  - looking to answer a specific question; and
  - looking to explore an area of concern.

- Get 'emergency' help, typical task sets might include:
  - checking what specific symptoms, or behaviour, in a child could mean;
  - urgent seeking of specialist (obviously some types of emergency may require the ambulance ...
  - ... although as monitoring technologies evolve, this currently very high concern mode will be able to be catered for automatically).

- Obtain a recommendation or trusted opinion, typical task sets might include:
  - checking up on quality, reputation of desired service; and
  - looking for more general thoughts and ideas with regard to a possible need.

Marketspaces and Modal Analysis
Taking these generic activities and coupling them with the list of tasks supported by the marketspace that will have been derived

from Modal Analysis we can build a step-by-step task list for each activity (for more on tasks, see p. 92).

For example the activity 'Get emergency help' above might involve seeking a medical specialist. Completing the Modal Analysis for this task for a moderately experienced customer we might derive the following task sequence.

Tasks in order of performance for 'seeking of a medical specialist'

1 Navigate to 'emergency assistance' in the 'expert advice' area of the marketspace.
2 Assess and compare specialists based upon specific mode (including location).
3 Obtain *trust* satisfaction (e.g. on reputation basis) using expert/ community references.
4 Create trusted shortlist.
5 Create final shortlist from trusted/approved pool.
6 Contact shortlisted specialists with requirement details.
7 Assess and compare initial responses.
8 Select final candidate.
9 Open detailed dialogue about specific needs with final candidate.

We can visualise these detailed tasks at a high level as a journey through the marketspace. Referring to our diagram of a marketspace, we can track the route through its resources that some of the task sets we identified involve, as illustrated in Fig. 7.2.

Note that we have illustrated two activities, 'getting "official" advice' and 'reconfigure automation requirements' as having

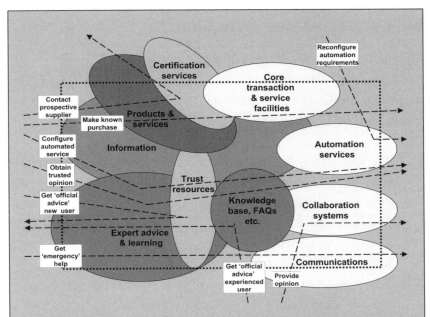

Fig. 7.2 Typical customer routes across a marketspace, according to purpose.

two potential paths, one for new customers who use 'information' and 'expert resources' perhaps to find their way around, the other for more experienced users who might approach the activity more directly. 'Provide opinion' by contrast will probably only be used by experienced users. Multiple potential paths are common and reflect degree of familiarity as an element of the customer's contextual mode.

Thus Modal Analysis reveals how marketspaces will actually be used. In turn, consideration of the marketspace components ensures that the analysis takes account of the full range of potential user resources. Even before we consider how it creates and maintains value, the marketspace configuration encourages us to think holistically about the customer's concerns.

Beating 'silo syndrome' in marketspaces

Solving the three problems of fragmentation

Customers, as we noted in Chapter 3, currently experience a high degree of inefficiency and dissociation in the Commoditised Internet, and this occurs across three dimensions.

1   The lack of support for purposive activity and coherent task sets, in the context of an ocean of information that largely fails to enable either meaning or trust, creates both *extra work and extra risk* for customers. They become single-handedly responsible for assigning their own meaning and trust to the information they encounter.

2   This problem is further compounded by the chasms of meaning and trust that lie between the – often individually useful – offerings of diverse business models such as niche product marketers and portals. We described earlier the phenomenon of *'island-hopping' between isolated chunks of value.*

3   The plethora of channels and access devices (which will naturally rationalise over time) tends to further encourage fragmentation of customer task sets, as customers are enabled (while at the same time restricted by the limitations of new devices ...) to *perform certain isolated functions without reference to a contiguous task set.*

How will marketspaces address each of these issues?

The keystone of Modal Analysis

We're assuming here that customers' critical routes through the marketspace – i.e. the components they encounter and the order in which they do so, according to their purpose and the derived task sets – will be anticipated through the application of Modal Analysis techniques. It's critical to grasp to what extent this approach will form the glue that pulls together what would otherwise be the familiarly fragmented elements of a customer experience, lacking either meaning or trust.

However, the Modal Analysis work alone does not guarantee a positive experience – the following concerns also need to be addressed:

- The degree to which the customers can clearly identify the focus of the concern or interest being addressed and the boundaries of what is encompassed. Lack of definition in these respects will destroy the ability to make sense of the offer and therefore the meaning of what is encountered.
- The completeness of the offer and the neutrality of the advice and selection process.
- The quality of its individual components and the manner in which they interact is also of course critical to the perceived value.

OTHER ESSENTIAL FEATURES OF MARKETSPACES
Focus

Marketspaces will address particular areas of customer interest or concern. They may be broad, as those dealing with health or domestic matters would be, or relatively restricted, focused on classical music for example.

The focus may include more than one domain of user concern. In the worked GoKids example above, Christopher uses it purely as a support to parenting, while Janet is additionally using it to support her professional concerns. For Christopher it lies in a personal domain we may call 'childcare at home' and includes relevant components from the related domain of healthcare. For Janet the coverage of a domain of her professional life, call it 'child development and education', may be as important, or more so (Fig. 7.3).

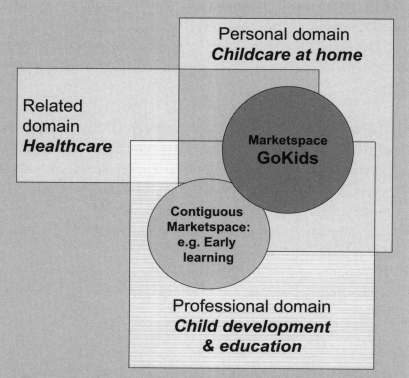

Fig. 7.3 Visualising domain and focus for marketspaces. Note that we have added a related marketspace 'Early learning' that may lie largely in the professional domain that is Janet's concern.

Boundaries

Focus addresses one element of the identity of a marketspace, but identity, and with it meaning, can be undermined by lack of clarity about the scope of the service. Marketspaces will need to establish boundaries, as far as possible ones that are natural to the subject matter, and communicate these clearly to customers.

Completeness and neutrality

Nothing undermines the validity of a customer-centred service offer more quickly than partiality. For a marketspace to be accepted and effectively carry out its tasks of making sense of the subject matter and reducing the information load on customers, reassurance that, within reason, all aspects of the concern and all relevant products and services are available is essential. If the customer must look elsewhere to seek reassurance that they have the complete background or the full range of solutions, the marketspace will have failed in a primary task (accepting that some customers will always want a second opinion does nothing to reduce the obligation).

Equally, observable bias, other than that expressed by independent experts or supported by external, validating evidence, immediately undermines trust. Thus a marketspace must perform the difficult feat of balancing neutrality at the general, service level with the opportunity for suppliers to present their offers in the best light, once particular solutions have been identified.

KEY POINT
Mode, marketspaces and getting beyond Silo Syndrome
Working through our three problems of fragmentation above:

1   *The* 'extra work and risk' *experienced by customers in the Commoditised Internet are reversed: Modal Analysis enables the marketspace to facilitate the customer's route across just those components that fit the current purpose, and the components combine to support the rapid attainment of meaning and trust. Note in particular the roles of 'expert advice' and 'learning and trust resources'. (Refer to the worked example on page 137, and also to Figure 7.2, to see step-by-step accounts of typical purposes and task execution.)*

2   *The* 'island-hopping' *experience of the Commoditised Internet will be replaced – again based upon Modal Analysis and quality of the components – with the delivery of a completely different type of encounter with the businesses within the marketspace. Quality offerings – exclusively of a highly relevant nature – will be met by the customer in a manner that addresses their current purpose, in a context that maximises meaning and trust: good for the customer, and of course ideal for businesses, who here will be optimally positioned to sell their services. (It's worth noting here, though, that not all marketers will be comfortable with this model of customer encounter – it can feel out of control, in that the customers comes to the brand, rather than the reverse.)*

3   *The* 'modal imperative' *of enabling coherent task sets to be executed as far as possible through one device type, across all relevant marketspace components, will minimise the* 'fragmentation of functions'.

TRUSTPOINT IDENTIFICATION (AN EXTENSION OF MODAL ANALYSIS)

Modal Analysis is a powerful method for establishing the critical tasks that customers must perform. On its own, however, it may fail to fully reveal the trust building requirements of the service. This is so because many of the types of reassurance that a customer requires are optionally accessed: they do not lie on the main task path, but are made available as separate consultable resources as required. Forcing customers to view even critical trust resources on every visit is counterproductive, indeed interruptive, defeating its own objective. So identification of the critical trustpoints discussed and identified in Chapter 5 needs a parallel, verifying analysis.

TRUSTPOINT IDENTIFICATION IN ACTION

Trustpoint identification is approached by listing the individual steps of the task sequence and assessing the need for supporting trust features. Table 7.1 provides an introduction to the technique for the hypothetical purpose within the GoKids marketspace that we explored earlier, 'seeking urgent help from a medical specialist'.

Table 7.1 Example of trustpoint identification process.

Tasks in order of performance	Component employed	Is this a Trustpoint?	Trust Resource provided
Navigate to 'emergency assistance' in the *Expert Advice* area	Expert system within Expert Advice	Y	Fast navigation (Recognition of purpose) Certification of information source (Reputation of service)
Assess and compare specialists based upon specific mode (incl. location)	Directory of experts and location tools		
Trust satisfaction (e.g., on reputation basis) using expert/community references	Trust resources & Knowledge base	Y	Independent certification of qualifications and customer experience (Reputation and Reassurance)
Create trusted shortlist	Shortlisting and bookmarking tolls from Marketspace facilities		
Create final shortlist from trusted/approved pool	–		
Contact shortlisted specialists with requirement details	Communications, and collaboration systems		
Assess and compare initial responses	Trust resources & own knowledge		
Select final candidate	–	Y	Evidence of suitability (Reputation and Reassurance) Specialists own activity (Response)
Open detailed dialogue about specific needs with final candidate	Communications, and collaboration systems		

Urgent seeking of a medical specialist

HOW MARKETSPACES PLAY OUT FOR BUSINESSES

We noted in Chapter 3 how almost all business approaches suffer irretrievable problems of value in the Commoditised Internet. While certain of these models may survive in the future – assuming they're able to find a context that enables meaning and trust – most will need to reassess their strategies dramatically in order to benefit at all from opportunities in digital markets.

The core problem is what we have, perhaps provocatively, called 'the reverse Midas touch'. The Internet's cold transparency and immediacy tends to strip value away from most offerings, while the primary source of new digital value – information – is disabled from adding value through a chronic lack of relevance and task-focus.

How then will marketspaces enable businesses to find their feet again?

Product and service providers

Ironically, in that they were often perceived as the most obvious beneficiaries of the e-commerce revolution, suppliers of goods and services seem to have suffered most in the Commoditised Internet. As we discussed earlier, almost all entrants have found it very difficult to gain leverage from either least cost or differentiation stances, due again to this commoditising transparency.

Marketspaces have the ability to attach relevant information to products and services, driven by the clear understanding of customer need that is conferred by Modal Analysis. They will thereby bring back a powerful form of value to product markets, benefiting in particular those providers whose offerings are high in customer concern and require a greater depth of information, such as childcare, healthcare, financial services and hobbies.

KEY POINT

Product offerings will be given an appropriate role and introduced at the required stage in the satisfactory execution of the customer task set. Meaning and trust will be enabled by the clustering of relevant information and related services (in particular expertise and specialisation) around products and services, to bring value back. Differentiated offers especially will be enabled – at least for products or services where information can add value.

The benefits of a new eco-system

Many product and service vendors will also be able to extend their offerings into a theoretically unlimited range of marketspaces, taking full advantage of the

Modal Analysis work hopefully performed by the owners of these marketspaces, to achieve maximum benefit (through optimal location in customers' task sets) with a pleasingly minimal outlay.

It is worth noting here however that luxury brands – which generally fail to gain from this attachment of relevant information to their offer, perhaps because in a sense they are perceived as, or need to be, somehow self-contained and complete – will remain at risk from the reverse Midas touch, and need to approach their stances in marketspaces with care.

Content owners

We looked closely at the problems of content in Chapter 5 ('Meaning, Trust and Value'). We identified content as being one of the earlier villains of the Commoditised Internet, in that without an approach that enabled customers to make sense of information and to minimise risk, it actually creates both extra work and risk for customers. 'Content is king' has clearly emerged as a rather fatal mantra.

In the marketspace environment, however, their positioning alongside both 'trust resources' and 'experts and specialists' in the marketspace environment will set up a strong platform for meaning and trust, that brings to the content owner not only a new and powerful customer value, but also a respectable position in the marketspace hierarchy in terms of partnership relationships with other businesses.

Finally, as with products and services, content owners will be able to operate profitably by participating in a wide range of marketspaces if they wish to.

KEY POINT

In marketspaces, content owners will be given a completely new lease on life. With the high degree of relevance achievable through Modal Analysis, and a presence within a contiguous set of other complementary component businesses, they will be rescued from the value-eroding position they had previously occupied. The value of some forms of information will indeed become so great that its owners are enabled to take a substantial portion of the revenue that arises from automated services depending on it.

Experts and learning providers

Owners of expertise will occupy an enviable role, in that they more than any other players occupy the high ground of both meaning and trust. The several forms of expertise that can leverage value from marketspaces are explored in detail in Chapter 9, 'Roles and Benefits in Marketspaces'

KEY POINT

The knowledge that experts bring provides the depth, neutrality and validation that are so often missing in digital markets. While many are readily accessible as independent services available for consultation, the additional effort of locating and enlisting their services is one of the symptoms of fragmentation in the Commoditised Internet. Relocation within marketspaces solves this problem to the benefit of both parties.

but, in what must be becoming a familiar pattern, they will all benefit primarily from the connectedness that integration of their services into the customer experience provides.

Infrastructure providers

A feature of marketspaces that must have become apparent is the need for substantial enabling infrastructure in the form of tools and systems. These are required both to support functionality and to enable delivery across a range of channels.

The need for infrastructure providers to connect, integrate and rationalise the many applications required to build and operate a marketspace points clearly to new, and sizeable, development opportunities.

TO SUMMARISE

- Marketspaces will feature a range of common components, that are varied according to the focus and boundaries of the business.
- They will solve the central customer value problem of 'silo syndrome' by:

- minimising work and risk for customers;
- positioning the components of the space optimally to provide an ideal route through it, reflecting and supporting key customer purposes and task sets; and
- enabling the use – as far as possible – of single channels and devices across entire task sets.
- Equally, marketspaces will resolve value problems for businesses by:
  - making information relevant to customer purpose, thereby supporting not only content owners but also product and service providers;
  - enabling content owners, product and service providers and experts, and learning providers to exploit opportunities at the optimal points in the customer experience; and
  - also enabling them to place their offerings across a range of spaces in diverse industry sectors, according to relevance and individual strategy.

CHAPTER 8

The Key Drivers and Enablers of Marketspaces

'I'm a great hand at inventing things. Now, I daresay the last time you picked me up, that I was looking rather thoughtful?'

'You were a little grave', said Alice.

'Well, just then I was inventing a new way of getting over a gate – would you like to hear it?'

'Very much indeed', Alice said politely.

IN THIS CHAPTER WE LOOK AT

- the technical trends that actively support the development of marketspaces, including:
  - the peer-to-peer, distributed computing model (P2P);
  - Extensible Markup Language (XML);
  - always-on channels;
  - automated services and 'triggers';
  - intelligent agents and 'bots'; and
  - recent experience in Business to Business (B2B) markets.

THINGS WE WON'T BE TALKING ABOUT IN THIS CHAPTER ...

Analyses of the technical drivers and enablers in digital markets unfortunately tend to focus upon several tried and true (and not always that relevant ...) developments. Before we get into the key issues, therefore, let's take a quick look at these.

The network effect

The tendency for the value of a network to increase as the square of the number of users is well understood, and has been an important driver of the Internet and businesses based on it. Indeed, in relative terms, only a limited portion of those who could be connected are: there's a long way to go even in some developed countries.

However, while we would not deny the importance of network effects in the initial establishment of digital markets, it is clear that the threshold of critical mass has long since been passed except in very specific sectors. In fact, the volume of users of the network, and the uses to which they want to put it, are now bumping against the limits of the original architecture. For the purposes of businesses, numbers of network connections are not the issue any longer. The focus needs to be upon the interactions that can be enabled, and where the business sits in respect to the community it enables.

Processor speed and bandwidth

Pushing the boundaries of the possible

Clearly some applications are enabled only if the available bandwidth, usually that of the customer's connection, can handle the volume of information sufficiently quickly and the receiving device can process it. Thus uses such as video and virtual reality have continuously been limited by these factors. However, the number of potential businesses that are really inhibited by lack of power or speed are few, except in the wireless world where bandwidth remains a severe limitation, pending the arrival of third generation mobile services.

As we examine later, increasing capacity to handle large media files represents a siren song for many businesses, which use it either to develop services 'because we can' with little underlying value generation, or to further frustrate customer purpose with irrelevant, off-task content.

User satisfaction

For most business purposes, processor speed and bandwidth impact primarily on the customer experience. Slow downloads and excessive demands on older processors create immense frustration and, as we saw in Chapter 1, immediate damage. The continued, if slow, roll-out of broadband, and the coming generation of mobile services are critical to addressing download speeds and overall satisfaction with digital service. In this restricted sense bandwidth is an enabler.

However, businesses have only themselves to blame when they fail to take account of current restrictions, and deliver content that creates bottlenecks and renders the experience worse than it might have been. For most purposes increased processor speed or bandwidth availability are not key determinants of success.

HARD HAT AREA!!

THE DYNAMIC DUO: P2P AND XML

P2P and the decline of server-dominated digital markets

The rapid adoption of the peer-to-peer model (see Fig. 8.1) sets up a central technical enabler for the evolution to marketspaces. Where e-commerce on the Commoditised Internet typically

HE SAID ... SHE SAID...

'Peer-to-peer networking – brought to international attention by the Napster music sharing system – is bounding into the corporate mainstream. Dozens of companies are now finding innovative applications for the technology.

Peer-to-peer networking is fundamentally different from the way in which Internet-connected computers normally send and receive information. Rather than computers retrieving information (such as music or software files) from central computers, peer-to-peer networks allow machines to share files without ever having to connect to a central source: files sitting on the hard disk of anyone signing up to a network can be downloaded by any other member.'

Net Profit Europe, January 2001.

spawned owned, standalone Web sites that were 'visited' by customers, the reduction in the need for client-server computing promotes a new customer empowerment that, among other impacts, makes the current 'destination' Web site model more or less irrelevant, as long as one can:

- make sense of what's out there in the market;
- find the appropriate resource; and
- connect to that resource with ease.

As a consequence, P2P will expose many product and customer aggregation services as inadequate, by enabling customers to perform these services for themselves and among each other.

This evolution is both facilitated and propelled by the evolving technical toolkit. The already extensive adoption of the XML standards for development, and emerging enablers such as SOAP (Simple Object Access Protocol) and UDDI (Universal Descrip-

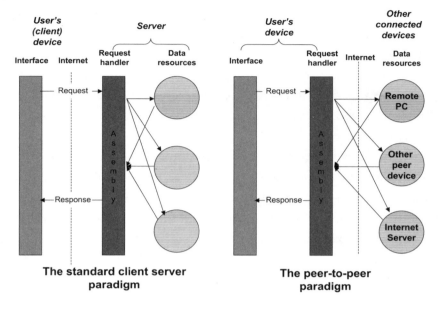

Fig. 8.1 A simplified comparison of the client server and peer-to-peer configurations. Peer-to-peer allows the entire range of connected devices on the network to become data resources.

tion, Discovery and Integration) all have the potential to return application power to the desktop.

Harnessing intelligent agents and specialised bots to this reinforced customer control, completes a formidable set of applications, placing the power to manage core services right into the customers' hands.

XML and the new meaning

What is it about XML (Extensible Markup Language) that makes it so difficult to explain its importance to the construction of digital markets? Perhaps an over-focus on technical issues related to the language (and the complexities accompanying its early adoption in a B2B context), matched by a lack of attention to what XML above all else brings to the table.

XML brings meaning. Meaning to business overall, in the sense that it supports the relatively rapid evolution, application and sharing of ownable sets of ontologies (or naming conventions, if you like) and business rules that streamline communications, and execute and validate transactions within companies, industry sectors, and to some extent the related sets of those industry sectors.

It brings meaning to individual businesses in that, as long as the specific ontologies of the sector in question are observed, their own company-specific business rules can be developed and usefully applied in the knowledge that they share common communication foundations with others.

XML brings meaning to customers too. Referring back to our thoughts on P2P above, XML-based applications at the terminal enable customers to determine, with an unprecedented degree of control and accuracy, not only precisely what they wish to find out about, but also exactly how and when (and note the degree of timely relevance that's created here …) that information is to be provided to them.

As we discuss later, a central responsibility and benefit for owners of marketspaces will be the development of the particular ontologies and business rules that frame the creation of value, trust and meaning for both partners and customers. The XML tools to enable this are already being established and tested.

How P2P and XML enable marketspaces

What dynamics do P2P and XML thus set up in digital markets, in terms of customer behaviour, customer expectation, loyalty, and the delivery of value by businesses?

Marketspaces as 'optimised clusters of meaning'
Despite the theoretical customer empowerment that these two important enablers bring, unsupported task sets in fact only en-

sure satisfactory outcomes when the collective or public context is correctly understood. Otherwise, they return us to the world of fragmented information, and the unmet customer need to 'make sense'.

Most of the customers, most of the time, will require the meaning that marketspaces provide, to provide both clarity, and the confidence that their purposive interactions are 'recognised' and fulfilled. In this sense, the marketspace is both mentor and guarantor for the customer, creating a communicable framework of meaning for the environment, and minimising the risk of misunderstanding.

KEY POINT

Marketspaces will emerge, grow and crystallise around a set of shared ontologies and business rules. They will thus bring together and maintain, in each instance, a highly fertile common context and infrastructure – 'an environment of optimised business meaning', if you like.

Partnerships of unprecedented flexibility and sophistication

To accomplish this, a marketspace environment will typically contain, balance and manage the multiple components we identified in Chapter 7.

Creating the common ontologies and business rules that enable the performance of all key communications and transactions within the marketspace, and support the emerging P2P marketplaces, produces a highly flexible business eco-system, within and around which, partners of all appropriate types can join forces.

In managing this eco-system, businesses can optimise their own individual benefit from meaningful exposure to – and engagement with – a focused and therefore highly valuable customer set. At the same time they ensure that the comprehensive and boundaried context for meaning that the marketspace represents, meets as many of the customers' potential requirements as possible.

In other words, no more isolation for the business, no more island-hopping for the customer.

ALWAYS-ON, MOBILE AND AUTOMATION

The real impacts of always-on

It's easy to underestimate always-on as simply a 'step-up from dial-up' – dial-up without the hassle, if you like.

But if the time-value of key decision-enabling information comes into our picture, we immediately see that always-on equips the customer – in particular when available through mobile device types – with an entirely new type of control over their interaction with digital markets.

In the previous predominantly dial-up environment, customers have been able – in a limited fashion at least – to configure online services such as news delivery or stock portfolio updates to PC or PDA, collect the results regularly, browse them for relevant items, and then perhaps to take some decisive action.

KEY POINT

Always-on creates a much higher potential customer value for both information, and the system that delivers it, by incorporating real-time events and information into the task set that the customer needs to execute.

With always-on, however, the real-time delivery of this type of information tends to dramatically increase its value, not merely due to its timely delivery, but more importantly because, assuming that the channel and device supports this, the customer can immediately take action. When I receive notification that my bid has been accepted in the auction for that *objet de desir*, I can immediately take action to secure it

This is in many ways the promise of interactive business finally made real, and we can note once again how our marketspace, with its cluster of meaning, its contiguous services, infrastructure and carriers, its expertise and content and its customer communities, plays so neatly to always-on.

PEER-TO-PEER IN A WIRELESS WORLD

To understand the power of these tools (as the increasing use of Java applications in mobile devices brings them together) consider a possible scenario in the not too distant future. Janet is working with her class on an assignment out of doors. They are studying natural history in a highly frequented but relatively inaccessible nature reserve. One of her class has a seizure. Obviously Janet calls for the emergency services in the usual way, but their location is relatively remote and she wants to take as much immediate action as possible.

Using her wireless-enabled PDA, Janet initiates a general enquiry routine that hunts all the local wireless devices (initially those within the current cell) for one whose owner's details, or electronic visiting card, indicate a medical doctor, and rings the device. An immediate link between the doctor's mobile and Janet is established, enabling her to request emergency assistance.

But we also need to note how always-on necessitates a clear, purpose- and task-based analysis of, and strategy for, the use of channels and devices. Without this, the sense of meaning and 'flow' for the customer that marketspaces can offer, are critically fragmented either because the task set becomes discontinuous or the continuity of the service experience is not maintained.

Automation, or how customer tasks disappear

It is a remarkable paradox that the information that is likely in tomorrow's marketspaces to represent most real commercial value to the customer, is that which is not directly experienced by the customer at all. We have become used to the increasing sophistication of software, the proliferation of devices and indeed the rising flood of customer engagement with digital markets, to the point where the rapid increase in automated functions, as part and parcel of customer service and business value, is easy to ignore.

But let's look at this more closely. Today's typical conscious customer task in the Commoditised Internet is performed step-by-step through a range of branded interfaces with hopefully adequate usability. As the systems that can perform this work become configurable by the customer, the work can increasingly as a result (perhaps 'triggered' by one of the real-time events referred to above) be automatically performed by the system on behalf of the customer.

Information (perhaps a combination of contextual expertise and real-time news or data) combines with the customer's pre-configured setting ('If and when this event occurs, I'll want you to do this, and then tell me you've done it…') and of course the appropriate software, to create what we call a 'trigger.' The principal outcomes are that:

- the work has been done by the (obviously trusted) system on behalf of the customer without requiring any customer work or time; and
- especially in the case of a task reflecting an important purpose, the action has been taken instantly, therefore in many critical situations maximising benefit and minimising exposure to risk.

These combine to create a value for the service that will soon leave the previous conscious, customer-driven task model behind.

This then becomes the new standard, a 'threshold facility' that a marketspace must have in order to be worth consideration by the promiscuous customer.

The new value of information

Why is this interesting to content owners (and also to 'owners of expertise')? Because, outside certain entertainment markets, content has struggled mightily to find its value in digital markets. Indeed, except in the context of learning or entertainment it is, as we said above, typically experienced by the customer as a liability rather than as an asset.

KEY POINT

In this new model, information achieves, if you like, the highest possible degrees of value for the business and for the customer. Making sense is most certainly enabled; purpose and mode are met with minimal inconvenience. Key tasks are supported, decisions are prompted, and repetitive, low-value work is minimised.

The consequently high value this type of automated service enables, by bringing tasks and information together in real-time, supports a true and sustainable commercial return for the business and a level of customer commitment that many 'loyalty schemes' can only dream about.

Always-on and automation in marketspaces

When always-on and automation come together, the impact is dramatically increased.

With the collaboration of the customer in an ongoing configuration and refinement process, a system that supports expertise, information and 'triggering' actions can take on a growing responsibility for complex analysis, low-concern (and eventually higher-concern) decision-making and tasks, and enquiry (i.e. 'bot-type') activities, on their behalf, or at least with their minimal involvement.

The customer's involvement in low-value, time-costly work is reduced further over time, and his or her interaction with the system occurs, therefore, at typically less frequent but increasingly important points in the contact cycle.

Marketspaces play uniquely to the combination of always-on and automation, by bringing together, within an environment of a shared ontology and set of business rules, comprehensive,

ALWAYS-ON AND AUTOMATION IN ACTION

We established earlier that one of Christopher's interests is classical music. We might imagine him belonging to a marketspace that not only enables him to purchase recordings, books and tickets but also provides regular news and features and keeps him in contact with peers who share his interest.

Christopher's special passion is baroque music, and concerts by certain performers are a must for him to attend. His marketspace is configured to notify him immediately when such concerts are scheduled. Unfortunately he is already engaged on the night of a major performance and has passed up the opportunity to make advance bookings. Only when the concert is already sold out is his original engagement cancelled. Christopher messages his peers to enquire as to whether they have spare seats and draws a blank; so he configures a tool in his marketspace to monitor for any tickets offered, and buy them at once below a certain threshold price or call him immediately if that threshold is exceeded.

A week before the performance Christopher receives a call notifying him that two tickets are available, but they are being offered at an inflated price somewhat above his threshold. Knowing that for this event he has only a short window of opportunity, Christopher can decide whether to close the deal at once or hope that other cheaper offers become available.

contiguous and meaningful facilities that support the provision of this type of value.

More simply, they can take the customer from information to action and back again, with both minimal effort and maximum relevance.

ENABLING AUTOMATED CUSTOMER VALUE WITH 'TRIGGERS'

What is a trigger?

A trigger is, in this context, a message that is created within a marketspace that either notifies a customer of an event and requests an action from the customer, or prompts an automated action by the system on behalf of the customer. In each case, the high-level components of the trigger are:

- the software that is used by the marketspace to hold and act upon informational elements and customer preferences;
- the information source from which the informational context for the trigger is derived;
- the news or update facility which delivers the 'change in circumstances' that, in combination with the informational context, delivers the variables for the trigger; and
- finally, the unique customer thresholds, or settings, (typically taking the form, at their most basic, of conditional 'If x, then y' statements) that establish the conditions under which the customer requires an action to be generated.

The ability to work with triggers marks one of the significant differences between always-on multi-channel markets and the World Wide Web delivered through the PC.

Why customers' complete task sets must be considered

In order to create this type of value for customers, a marketspace needs to offer a contiguous set of services that are complete for the purpose in hand. In other words, services that enable the customer to perform tasks in one environment, in one sequence, and using the most convenient device.

EXAMPLES OF SIMPLE TRIGGERS

In an auctioning environment, triggers would be used to alert the customer to an acceptance of their offer for a particular product: 'We can offer you a round-trip flight to Sydney for only $300.' They may also be configured to offer the opportunity to make a decision: 'I accept your offer of £3.50 for my treasured Manchester United pencil case', for instance.

In a financial management marketspace, triggers would alert customers to shifts in their stocks. Customers will in many instances configure the trigger to perform a reactive automated function at the moment a threshold is crossed, to minimise risk and/or maximise benefit. This would take the form of ' If x occurs, do y, then notify me that this has been done.'

For example, checking share prices and predictions is part of a larger purpose, i.e. managing a share portfolio. In an always-on environment this activity is both an on-demand one and a response to triggers.

In an environment assisted by automation it has several steps each of which may be an entry point (Fig. 8.2):

1   responding to a channel alert (trigger);
2   checking movements, pundits and charts;
3   adjusting the portfolio; and
4   setting monitoring levels and requesting alerts.

INTELLIGENT AGENTS AND 'BOTS'

No round-up of the significant developments in the technical environment would be adequate without reference to intelligent agents and 'bots.' The best-known manifestations of these are probably shopping bots and 'smart' search engines. 'Bots' in this

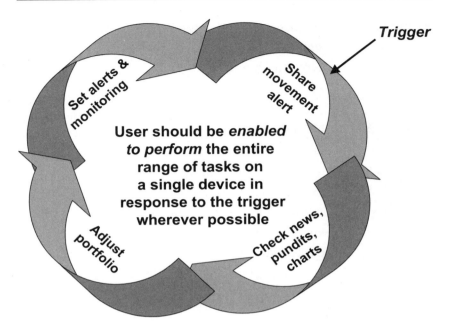

Fig. 8.2 The activity sequence in responding to automated triggers for the management of a share portfolio.

context can be considered as autonomous agents of the user that carry out specific tasks on the network and report back on the results. Thus shopping bots can provide continuous search functions looking for specific products by price or features.

'Smart' search engines can be trained by the user to recognise the contextual element of usage. They are not restricted to returning a list containing all references to a word or word-string, but can be progressively taught that, for instance, a search for the expression 'blue sky' is intended to return results referring to speculative research not the colour of the sky.

Although there is a considerable cross-fertilisation, in that new applications increasingly feature elements of both capabilities, there are two underlying concepts at work here:

- the ability to operate independently of the user's machine or a specific server; and

- the ability to progressively refine the functionality in response to the user's commands (and certain other external events) in a fashion that emulates learning.

AND BACK IN THE REAL WORLD ...

'UK-based Magenta Corporation uses artificial-intelligence techniques to create "smart agents" that can negotiate a sale or purchase according to pre-determined criteria. For example, a smart agent could be instructed to find and purchase a blue Ford Mustang* for the best possible price, to be delivered in the shortest possible time. The smart agents work using "fuzzy logic" and "partial matching". Fuzzy logic is a technique that can make sense out of statements or values that are in the grey area between "completely true" and "completely false". This allows them to make compromises during an automated negotiation.

'Partial matching is method of matching two sets of values (such as a seller's price and a buyer's offer) which partially – but may not completely – fit together. Using these two techniques, Magenta has built models for virtual marketplaces where thousands of smart agents – each with a specific "mission", such as buying a blue Ford Mustang as cheaply as possible – work in parallel, buying and selling from one another.'
Net Profit Europe, January 2001

*But what year? What condition? Engine size? Clearly not written by a car buff!

BLESSED ARE THE CHEESE-MAKERS ...

Janet has set a class project for the term on cheese and cheese-making but she knows that the materials available from the usual providers of learning materials are rather dry and academic and therefore unlikely to engage the children. She wants to find ways of bringing the subject to life and has used a specialised researching tool provided by GoKids to find supporting materials.

This tool is both an intelligent agent and a 'bot' that has been part-configured for the task. It enables her to automatically exclude online sites and resources that are inappropriate for the age group, and its configuration and 'training' already include the ability to specify subject areas and limit searches to approved resources if so desired. Its interface also allows her to extend the search beyond the 'official' sites and recognised bodies that are included in its default settings and to pre-configure many of the contextual and associative clues that indicate the type of results she is seeking. After entering appropriate initial settings, she will still need to refine its activity by responding to the first results suitably, but shortly she can let it perform an extended Internet crawl in the knowledge that a high percentage of the results will be relevant to her purpose.

Using this mechanism Janet finds, among a range of options, a number of suppliers who offer samples of cheese types including cow, sheep and goats' milk cheeses that employ different production processes including Cheddaring and Blue Veining. These samples come with scientifically and nutritionally sound information packs and can be ordered by the children or their parents. Additionally, she finds a number of useful online resources, including an animated game made to support a Dutch educational programme that challenges its users to turn raw milk into cheese against the clock, but requires them to employ scientifically sound steps and constituents to do so. The tool has dramatically reduced her search work over that of the usual search engine, which would have returned tens of thousands of results.

Thus she is supported in enlivening her classes and assignments by using tools that are easily refined for the task and will retain many of her settings.

These characteristics increasingly enable behind-the-scenes development that dramatically extends the capabilities and operation of the network. Direct customer use has, however, tended to be restricted to very simple tasks. This is because on their own, as with so much on the Internet, they lack context and are for many customers literally incomprehensible. Only by connecting them to the customer's mode in a marketspace environment does their use become obvious, and their adoption for quite sophisticated tasks become probable.

THE INFLUENCE OF BUSINESS-TO-BUSINESS

Three components of recent business-to-business developments contribute strongly to the enabling framework and may, in themselves, be drivers of a change in trading patterns.

Infrastructure

We have already seen that the best-known business-to-business initiatives, supply chain improvements, often based on hubs and exchanges, are efficiency enhancements and not value enhancements, but this is not the whole story. These developments drive the formulation of the sector-based ontologies we mentioned earlier, and they provide the flexible communications structure that allows complete supply chains to be rapidly reconfigured. So they are critical shapers of the digital infrastructure that enables the potentially complex partnerships and trading patterns behind marketspaces.

Customer data

A second trend in business markets, installation and configuring of Customer Relationship Management (CRM) systems, has also been touched on in respect of the intrusive and value-destroying loyalty campaigns that they are so often used to implement. But on the positive side, accurate information about customers, their current status and their preferences is essential to any worthwhile digital service and to enabling customer interactions. Today's CRM systems once again form an important foundation for the future, though some questions remain about the interoperability of proprietary systems that may be storing up trouble and cost for the future.

Collaboration

The third, and in many ways most important, development in B2B markets is the genuine value enhancement being created with the growth of collaborative systems: enhancements to product development, shared operations and the management of joint projects. The importance here is not so much in the systems themselves but in their effect on company boundaries, whose fluidity is further increased, and on the speed with which joint operations can be initiated and transferred. Increasingly, dynamic production and marketing configurations improve the climate and enhance the chances of success for inherently co-operative ventures such as marketspaces.

TO SUMMARISE

- P2P and XML will combine to support marketspaces in the creation and delivery of meaning by businesses to customers, while at the same time facilitating the often complex business partnerships that feature in the new model.
- Always-on, mobile and automation will empower customers in fundamentally new ways, bringing information, real-time events and customer purposes and tasks together for the first time, to both reduce leg-work (especially where bots are in use) and dramatically improve control and responsiveness.

- Information will therefore achieve a far greater relevance and hence value to customers and owners, and the services around which the information is clustered will equally be assigned new, higher value.

CHAPTER 9

Roles and Benefits in Marketspaces

'Will you, won't you, will you, won't you, will you join the dance?'

IN THIS CHAPTER WE LOOK AT

- the opportunities for participation that the marketspace configuration creates for key types of business, focusing upon:
  - information providers,
  - directory services,
  - product and service suppliers,
  - experts, learning providers and brokers, and
  - advertisers;
- the contribution, roles, relative leverage and benefits that each participant achieves; and

- the implications of the marketspace configuration for retailers, manufacturers and financial service companies.

HOW TO APPROACH THIS CHAPTER

In this chapter and the next, we review the key outcomes of the marketspace approach for participants and management. As we find our way, along with thousands of others, towards the frameworks and vocabularies with which to address the new business realities of digital markets, we find ourselves working with models that have significant impact on the structure and conduct of business. These chapters explore that impact. Here we examine the effects from the perspective of participating companies, asking ourselves:

- What real value can the business contribute?
- What roles might that enable it to play?
- How much leverage would it have?
- Which benefits are thereby available?

We conclude this chapter with a brief examination of the implications and opportunities for some major business sectors. The next chapter goes on to explore the management issues, the relationship dynamics and the strategic benefits from the perspective of the owner.

Attempting to map existing, sector-based descriptions of business onto the marketspace roles, and then summarising the full range of opportunities for, for example a retailer, risks obscuring the issues. Instead we have approached this analysis by examining each major marketspace component in turn, and summarising the role and its associated benefits.

Readers may prefer to explore the roles that might be open to their organisation, and review the relevant parts of this chapter, rather than read each entry in sequence. Retailers, for instance, might consider exploiting their knowledge of products and the buying process in the role of independent expert, or their expertise in procurement as a broker, rather than look solely at the supply of products and services. Many roles may seem to offer opportunities but, in concluding that their business might play a multiplicity of the roles, readers should be wary of two potential sources of conflict:

1   It is essential to customer trust that expert advice be independent of any interest in the supply of solutions. The expert contribution to design of key customer support, as well as providing customer advice, is very substantial and its potential benefits equally so, but it often precludes other forms of involvement.

2   Some roles naturally create opposing dynamics; they exert pressures that pull the business towards a different emphasis and outcomes. This may have a healthy, balancing effect within a well-designed and managed configuration, but playing both could create internal conflicts for the participating company. (The issue of dynamics is explored further in the next chapter.)

Finally, if envisaging participation in a marketspace, readers might like to apply this simple rule-of-thumb: the value drivers of the marketspace should enable the value drivers of the participating company.

THE MAJOR COMPONENTS AND ROLES

To recap, we've identified the common core components that are brought together to form a viable marketspace as:

- information;
- certification services;

- expert advice and learning;
- products and services;
- trust resources;
- the knowledge base and FAQs;
- core transaction and service facilities;
- automation services;
- collaboration systems; and
- communication systems.

The management or owners will provide the last four of these, which become shared, common resources, and the knowledge base will grow as a consequence of operation. The first five give rise to the major internal roles that may be open to participating organisations; finally there are a number of external roles, for example advertisers or sponsors.

Take your partners ...

We have established that the provision of certification services, which necessarily constitute an external source of validation, and the providers of expert advice, must essentially remain independent of marketspace ownership and all other participants. It is also unlikely that a single company will be able to provide all the remaining components credibly, even in the unlikely circumstance that they have the capabilities and assets in-house to do so. First, the requirement to offer a representative range of competing products and services is a core trust consideration in every case, and is outside the remit of almost all organisations. Second, to undertake all of the remaining roles sets up core competence conflicts for most organisations, that are likely to undermine the quality of key components.

As a result, although at the time of writing most nascent marketspace-type ventures (like WebMD) are established by independents and typically venture-capital backed, the coming generation of marketspaces will often be initiated by partnerships or joint ventures between interested parties, who can provide elements of the mix. (Coalitions, however, do not remove the need for executive ownership to provide coherence and direction to the overall service proposition. These management issues are the subject of the next chapter.)

Generic roles in marketspaces

Although the precise components of each marketspace will vary depending on its focus and character, a variety of generic roles can be deduced from the above. These will be needed to supply one or more of the core components that will feature in the majority of marketspaces. They include:

- information providers;
- directory services;
- experts and learning providers;
- brokers;
- product and service suppliers; and
- advertisers.

Three further roles are of critical important to the marketspace, to provide credibility, accessibility and service optimisation. These are:

- certification services;
- enabling technology providers; and
- channel owners.

All three will usually come from external providers. Certification services will inevitably be particular to the marketspace and the domain of customer concern it addresses; the enabling technology will reflect its individual operational requirement. They will therefore not be explored here. Channel owners provide essential access for customers and are able to levy charges for that access; we have viewed these as management concerns and they are covered in the next chapter.

We will now review the major roles in turn.

INFORMATION OWNERS

The contribution of information owners

Many organisations, from publishers to utilities, own information that is of potential value to a marketspace. Some common types of information that will usually be required are shown in Fig. 9.1 (note that the trigger data for automation will be included under market-specific sources as will many other high-value components).

Roles for information owners

The essential contribution of information in marketspaces, and how it can be leveraged to earn a return, is better understood when the various ways in which it adds value are explored. In declining order of value, information owners can provide:

1   direct data flows that support automated and semi-automated services, especially for the provision of trigger information;

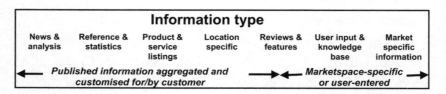

Fig. 9.1 Types of information that feature in a marketspace and their various roles for the customer.

2   high-value, market-specific data and news, particularly items that have time-value for customers (market prices and location specific or scheduling information);

3   raw data (such as electricity prices) as essential constituents of value-added services, customisable news, and pertinent contextual assistance (such as expert systems for decision support);

4   generic content and magazine material; and

5   occasional or contributory syndicated content.

Leverage and capture of economic value for information owners

Because information owners control access to essential elements of some of the most valuable services, those that are critical to customer retention, they potentially have relatively high leverage within the marketspace model. As a result they are good candidates as possible owners or part-owners (although publishers' drive to exploit information as broadly as possible through continual repurposing can create a tendency to pursue horizontal expansion at the risk of adequate vertical depth).

KEY POINT

Note that two of the potentially most valuable information categories, the information feeds supporting automated services, and the data that contributes to decision making, may not be directly accessible in marketspaces. Rather these components fluctuate with changing background events, and their current state becomes briefly visible when a response is required. Their value is entirely dependent on the customer's need.

Because trigger and decision-supporting information is so critical, information owners who have good coverage of marketspace requirements may be in a position to command much of the value accruing from automated services. But note that the timeliness of these services is so crucial, that wire services and the owners of raw data are in a more commanding position than media owners who repackage it.

The benefits for information owners

KEY POINT

Revenue models that have hitherto been hard to realise become feasible in the marketspace context. This ability to return value to information is a unique feature of the marketspace proposition, and provides information owners with reinforced leverage in these markets, as well as enhanced income.

For publishers the marketspace paradigm and its service features provide one of the few ways that they can leverage value in digital markets from their core product, rather than indirect revenue from advertising. Other owners of information can benefit from the high value that accrues to the data that is used to drive triggers, has contextual, time and location-based relevance, or supplies essential content for decision support.

REVENUE POTENTIAL FOR INFORMATION OWNERS

The following are revenue models that information owners might employ:

1 share of ownership of marketspace and therefore, potentially, of all revenues (especially where the value of their information is high);
2 partnership, alliance or contract for the supply of data to support high-value services such as automation;
3 participate in the marketspace to extend the reach of an existing revenue earning service;
4 charge for syndicated content;
5 obtain subscriptions or service referrals;
6 share in sponsorship or advertising income (but note that, whilst sponsorship of some services is viable, the pure advertising sales opportunity in marketspaces tends to be low, see advertisers later in this chapter); and
7 provide free content and receive onward traffic.

DIRECTORY SERVICES

The contribution of directory services

Directory services constitute a specific category of information provider, essentially distinguished by the completeness and organisation of their information. Their asset tends to be listings information, and again a variety of businesses other than dedicated companies may own valuable examples, some of which may be critical to the support of customer choice. Some common directory components are shown in Fig. 9.2.

Roles for directory services

The importance of the role played by directory services in marketspaces increases with the specificity of the marketspace, and its practical or emotional significance to the customer. Essentially they combine knowledge with navigation, helping customers to narrow their choice and select from a range of alternatives, and directing them to their chosen resources.

There is a further need in many markets for directories of complementary and supporting products and services – either because they are not suited to digital marketing, are too localised, or are provided by highly fragmented suppliers.

The nature and role of catalogues of commoditised products is examined under 'Product and service suppliers' below, but it can be noted that the e-tail concept, product marketing via catalogue on the Internet, is essentially a specialised directory service with minimal trust features.

Fig. 9.2 The types of directory that may feature in a marketspace.

Leverage and capture of economic value for directory services

Directory services constitute a key asset for many marketspaces, especially those where important services required by customers are provided locally or by many, fragmented suppliers. For example, in a marketspace that includes home services such as childminders, plumbers, electricians or builders, the directories and complementary trust resources become essential.

In certain marketspace models, a single directory service owner may provide a set of resources sufficiently critical to command a high degree of leverage, perhaps even part-ownership. However in the more general case, a range of contributors will provide directories, and their owners will need to settle for capturing value from the use of their services in some way.

The benefits for directory services

The primary advantage of the marketspace configuration for directory owners lies in the incorporation of their service into the customer value chain at the critical point when they are needed, rather than, as tends to be the case currently, as a separate and often disjointed task.

There are also opportunities that hold the promise of new sources of revenue and more meaningful customer engagement. These include increasing the utilisation of a directory by incorporating it into decision tools and semi-automated task sets that require the customer to select a supplier. There may also be opportunities to extend the value proposition by developing complementary trust services (this is not, however, a free ride, and is offset for most current directories by the considerable cost of incorporating the necessary validation services and the effect it may have on core subscription income). Customer subscriptions

> ## REVENUE POTENTIAL FOR DIRECTORY SERVICES
> Possible revenue sources will include:
>
> - share of ownership of marketspace and therefore, potentially, of all revenues (especially where the value of their information is high);
> - listing fees paid by the directory entrants;
> - referral fees paid by services booked through the directory;
> - participation in customer subscriptions for services that utilise directories; and
> - contract for the supply of marketspace-specific directory services.

for such services provide further potential revenue on top of listing and referral fees and ratings services.

EXPERTS, LEARNING PROVIDERS AND BROKERS

The contribution of experts, learning providers and brokers

Experts

Expert resources are at the heart of most successful marketspace propositions. Their input in terms of core processes for knowledge, decision support and just-in-time availability is a critical component of meaning and trust for customer task sets, and in many instances fulfils a set of tasks in its own right.

KEY POINT

So experts and learning providers cease to be isolated facilities (our 'islands of value') in the digital environment, and in marketspaces become instead key assets for delivery on the value proposition.

Three primary contributions have been alluded to earlier in this book: contributing to design of components of the infrastructure, provision of structured knowledge and active availability for consultation. Some of these

Fig. 9.3 Some of the contributions that experts can bring to a marketspace.

knowledge and accessibility characteristics are captured in Fig. 9.3.

Learning providers

In marketspaces, learning providers offer a particular form of structured expertise, where the customer is provided with the tools to absorb the knowledge necessary to provide a thorough grounding in the principles of a subject matter. Learning does not eliminate the need for other expertise, but it does equip the customer to make informed choices and provide the contextual background that ensures a shared understanding of less structured information.

Brokers

From the perspective of marketspaces, brokers are a special instance of experts who can provide market knowledge and transaction design. In those markets where they exist, they have unique insight and connections. In contrast to information providers, their primary contribution is in improving vertical depth, bringing both specialisation and insight to the customer. In return they may attract clients for the handling of complex sales or purchases.

Roles for experts, learning providers and brokers

The multiplicity of roles that experts may play is worth further exploration, they can:

- consult in the design and development of selection tasks and the knowledge and reference components of the marketspace;
- design and develop expert product configuration tools such as choice-boards;[1]
- design and develop expert systems to advise and support customers;
- provide generic advice within the marketspace;
- be available to provide real-time expert advice (by developing a special service or extending an existing one);
- provide asynchronous expert advice by responding to queries posted in discussion groups or by e-mail; and
- provide third-party expert advice to referred customers through their own service.

Learning providers will contribute similar knowledge and selection provision, but at one remove from the material about which the customer needs advice or decision criteria. By supplying structured educational components, they assist customers in making their own choices. The selection of learning, rather than concurrent advice, will often depend on the nature of the task; simple expert tools can support a one-off choice, but repetitive and risky decisions may require deeper knowledge.

Brokers and market makers of all sorts perform parallel functions. Their deep knowledge of the markets, and in many cases control of key transactions, make them critical to success in marketspaces featuring complex transactions, or where risk is offset by financial instruments.

Leverage and capture of economic value for experts, learning providers and brokers

Experts have high leverage within a marketspace. There are some niche markets or niche components of a larger market where experts and brokers have extensive or even exclusive knowledge and brand presence. However, if the knowledge is more widely distributed among a range of suppliers, this fragmentation reduces bargaining power.

Whatever the structure of the market for provision, experts are usually essential to the added value that a marketspace extends, but their participation in ownership can be problematic if their independence is not to be suspect. As the expert role shades towards brokerage (i.e. where deep knowledge and wide-ranging contacts are essential to the location and procurement of the solution) so the opportunity for ownership increases.

Learning providers have less leverage and will usually participate in a supplier role.

Benefits for experts, learning providers and brokers

Experts, consultants and brokers

For brokers as well as experts and consultants, a marketspace provides a contextual environment that aggregates customers who may otherwise be hard to attract to a standalone digital service, and it dramatically increases their reach in comparison with physically located services. As we have seen, the opportunities are multiple: supply and consultancy in respect of core expert knowledge and systems, branded or unbranded presence in the marketspace, and real-time and near-real-time consultancy.

REVENUE POTENTIAL FOR EXPERTS AND BROKERS

Apart from any participation in ownership both will be likely to operate under a service level agreement and receive some combination of fees, margins on sales or profit share, balanced against any opportunities they have for direct business with the customer.

Their revenue opportunities are correspondingly great, as are those for the creation of long-term relationships. They are enabled, in effect, to create a new relationship dynamic with existing customers and access to new customers, in addition to any service agreement with the marketspace. For brokers these opportunities naturally extend to their involvement in any transaction.

Learning providers

For learning providers, marketspaces reinforce the growing importance of integrating customer learning into the sales process. They provide an outlet for generic knowledge objects and bespoke learning, and potentially offer participation in the design of expert- and decision-support systems. At the same time would-be students of fuller learning courses can be exposed to the company's offer.

PRODUCT AND SERVICE SUPPLIERS

The contribution of product and service suppliers

A wide variety of products and services will be required for the satisfaction of the many purposes that customers will express within the typical marketspace. A full range of products appropriate to the domain is essential to the success of such a service. Figure 9.4 captures the physical type and delivery characteristics of the range of typical products and productised services that a marketspace might feature.

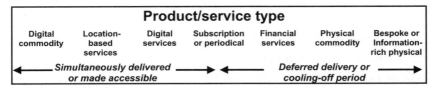

Fig. 9.4 Products and commoditised services distinguished by their delivery characteristics.

Within any marketspace, many of these products will be commodity items sold by third parties trading in the established fashion of the Commoditised Internet, who will view it as one of a range of outlets that extend their scale and reach, generating incremental revenue. We remarked above that this approach could be characterised as a type of directory activity, and it is indeed a close relative of mail order. While the participation of these companies is essential to ensure the availability and competitive pricing of simple products, this approach misses the potential richness of the contribution that suppliers who are more deeply involved can bring.

As we have noted, such a proposition will not work for more differentiated products. Marketers of such products need to participate more deeply in marketspaces, embedding them in the customers' task sets at the point of selection. In the next section we review some trends that powerfully affect the roles that are open to them, dramatically increasing their leverage, and more importantly their potential sales.

Roles for product and service suppliers

Approaching products from the commodity perspective and focusing on the transaction, leads us into thinking solely from the perspective of either enhancing the selling process (demand aggregation, benefits selling and so on) or optimising the purchasing experience (one-click purchase, choice-board customisation and so on). By engaging instead with the new perspectives on products and the benefits they bring, we gain a different understanding of the roles that may be open to product suppliers.

Typically, would-be marketers of differentiated products in digital markets have tended to distinguish them by their physical characteristics, inherent complexity, information content and ongoing support requirements. This helps in defining the sales process but still fails to capitalise on the real benefits of the digital market.

A fundamental change in perspective

To appreciate the range of opportunities open to marketers, we must review a major trend that has been at work within the broader marketplace for some time; a trend that is amplified in digital markets – the shift from value in the product to value in the service benefits that ownership brings.

One important insight is that, within marketspaces, customer task sets that involve purchase represent, for the marketer, only a portion of the customer cycle of interaction. Thus rather than just 'being present' in catalogues and product directories, products need to appear among the limited but representative and recommended range of relevant products, that is suggested when the appropriate step in the task sequence is reached.

This approach fundamentally alters the balance of drivers in digital markets: differentiated products, and particularly service-enhanced ones, now clearly stand to recover much of the value that is stripped away by the Commoditised Internet.

In a marketspace environment, they are able to both connect their benefits directly with consumer needs at the time of greatest opportunity and, in many cases, to enlist the support and endorsement of experts and expert systems.

However, this 'recovery of value' will apply only to products whose differentiation can be shown to provide real benefits. Higher price brands that rely on 'information asymmetries'[2] to

KEY POINT

This change affects the way both marketers and consumers view the product, and it extends powerfully across to the value-creating characteristics of digital services, underpinning successful participation by product marketers. It leads producers to see products as a platform for the delivery of services, and marketers to view the purchase as a single step in a fuller cycle of consumer interaction.

KEY POINT

A second insight is that the selection of a product is often only the initial stage of engagement, paving the way for the delivery of complementary products and services (in an appropriate and non-intrusive fashion). Those suppliers who can provide a wide range of support services may also be able to leverage them by extending their coverage to other products and to customer needs identified within the marketspace.

sustain a price premium will find it hard to seize these advantages, and are still liable to find themselves commoditised.

A SHIFT IN PERSPECTIVE ABOUT PRODUCTS

For ten or more years, value has been shifting from production ('the creation of things') to outcomes ('the benefits that ownership provides'). This trend can be seen in a number of developments, for example:

- A move towards temporary rental or longer-term leasing rather than outright ownership of some products.
- The increasing value of substitute services that replace the product (e.g. cleaning services rather than cleaning products).
- A growing tendency for products, especially larger infrequently purchased products, to be seen as platforms for services that become available after purchase.
- Many producers now view the product as a component of a longer customer value chain, one that consists of information and services clustered around the entire usage cycle. (Ownership of the product 'as an end in itself' is increasingly restricted to certain branded goods and subject to the vagaries of fashion; our promiscuous customer in their most virulent non-digital manifestation!) Thus many marketers now work to a lifecycle service model such as that in Fig. 9.5.
- Other businesses are starting to view such services as merely meeting threshold requirements and, as car manufacturers are doing, have moved on to consider the product as a platform for a range of post-sales and digital services. The car can theoretically be sold at or below cost, because the margin is delivered by post-sales service activity. (Note also here the degree to which information, as a basis for meaning and trust and as a core component of the services, becomes a fundamental component of the product.)

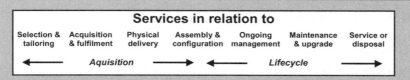

Fig. 9.5 Elements of the product lifecycle that may be enhanced by the addition of value-added services.

KEY POINT

To leverage marketspaces effectively, product marketers must approach them in this light, integrating the product sale into the customer value chain represented by the task sequence they are engaged with, and seizing the opportunity to add value in the form of digital services, whether supported by the marketspace or independently provided.

The ambiguous status of commodity products

Marketers of commoditised products face a potential dilemma. If they wish to benefit from marketspaces more fully than merely by obtaining impulse sales from a catalogue presence, they must enhance the information and trust components of the product, and devote effort to integrating it into the customer task sequence. But all of this has a cost, and when competing in a transparent market, this additional cost is unlikely to be sustainable and is furthermore not to the benefit of the marketspace, which needs to remain competitive in this respect.

So commodity products will either continue to appear in marketspaces in their most basic catalogue form (often as an embedded link), or they will need to be bundled with services so as to create a differentiated package of sufficient overall value to justify the price and the investment.

Role summary for product marketers

The above analysis serves to reveal the complexities of the product marketer's position, and the differing roles that are open to various players. Below, we use a broad classification, grouping potential suppliers by type to differentiate some obvious roles they may perform within the marketspace (ongoing services delivered directly by the marketer are excluded), but the distinctions are somewhat artificial and many roles cross these boundaries.

Commodity marketer roles

- Providing an integrated catalogue service aggregating commodity products within the marketspace.
- Presence within the marketspace as a link that refers customers to a separate service aggregating commodity products.
- As an intermediate, processing and fulfilling orders for branded goods, services or subscriptions placed within marketspace.

Producer roles

- Servicing orders placed direct through an exchange (with others in the marketspace arranging fulfilment).
- Using the marketspace to manage demand by disposing of excess inventory at competitive prices by, for instance:
  - direct sale of excess inventory in the marketspace;
  - auction of excess inventory in the marketspace;
  - responding to Requests for Quotation to fulfil aggregated demand; and
  - responding to a single customer's price offer.

Roles open to both producers and niche marketers

- The direct supply of physical goods from the producer or niche marketer as an integrated component of the selection task.

- The direct supply of digital products for download from either the marketspace or the supplier's servers, also as an integrated component of the selection task.
- Presence within the marketspace as a link that refers customers to a separate service marketing niche products.

Product-related service roles
- Providing delivery, installation and after sales services for a range of other suppliers.
- Co-development with the marketspace owners of automated services delivered through a product platform.

Leverage and capture of economic value for product and service suppliers

The above analysis suggests that the range of potential roles open to product marketers, from commodity supplier to extended service provider, will command different levels of leverage. Simplifying the categories we can observe the following.

Commodity products and services
These command little leverage in marketspaces, and since their attention is likely to focus primarily on the volume and reach of a restricted product range, they are unlikely to be concerned with participation in ownership. They are also easily substitutable, and therefore have leverage only if they are genuinely the lowest price providers. Commodity services such as finance for purchases, guarantees and fulfilment services are, however, important lubricants, and in this respect have greater significance.

Differentiated products
These have greater leverage, but differentiated products are unlikely to participate in ownership unless they cover a wide range of marketspace needs. Of more significance to them may be the option to lever-

age existing expert customer and product knowledge, to consult on development, or to supply expert knowledge in the marketspace.

Differentiated services

Differentiated services have still higher leverage and are, in some cases, possible owners or part-owners (consider some financial service organisations or art auctioneers). They may be more critical to the marketspace than any products and will be a primary source of possible future competitors. However, the disadvantage to them of marketspace ownership lies in the reformulation of their business required to concentrate on value-adding digital services: they would almost invariably need to allow their competitors into the structure of the broad offer, or risk undermining comprehensiveness and trust.

Benefits for product and service suppliers

Again we look at the different categories:

Commodity products and services

For commodity marketers, marketspaces are an additional outlet to extend reach and volume. They are driven to participate through need, since marketspaces will be where a significant volume of customers may be found, and if they decline to participate, a competitor will always do so.

Differentiated products and services

Marketspaces by definition offer access to a valuable, concerned customer base. Because the focus of the marketspace is on the details of the subject matter, and on finding an optimal (or satisfactory) solution, differentiated products stand to gain. The expert advice and decision support that are central to the marketspace model support their core proposition, by highlighting the advantages and 'fit' of the product.

REVENUE POTENTIAL FOR PRODUCT AND SERVICE SUPPLIERS

Product and service suppliers may capture value through a multitude of options including some of the more straightforward ones listed below:

- sales obtained through presence in market as extension of the brand reach, paying the marketspace owners either:
  – an agreed fee, or
  – a margin on sales;
- making sales on own service to referred customers for an agreed margin or fee;
- making marginal sales of excess inventory by using the marketspace as a demand management outlet;
- being a supplier to, or fulfilment partner of, the marketspace where goods are sold under the marketspace brand;
- being a wholesaler to the marketspace (where the marketspace or one of its members performs retail functions including fulfilment);
- selling complementary services bundled with their own products, those of other suppliers or products sold by the marketspace; and
- subscription sales for automated services developed with the marketspace.

For established producers who are hesitant to sell directly in online markets for fear of commoditisation devaluing their product, this may be one of the few digital sales channels they can benefit from.

ADVERTISERS

Roles for advertisers

The major disadvantages of interruptive advertising in digital markets have been clearly highlighted earlier. In most cases the negative impact on the customer experience outweighs the income advantages to a marketspace, which will be unwilling to accept advertising except within free, generic and low-value information (though the nature of a marketspace is such that this is necessarily limited).

There may be opportunities for the sponsorship of certain elements, especially of services and for the placement of advertising content if it adds real value. However, given the nature of marketspaces, most products that could benefit from exposure to an aggregated audience would benefit more from a fuller participation (i.e. in appropriate opportunities for encounter within the customer task set) and the direct sales that would arise.

Benefits to advertisers

Would-be advertisers who embrace the sponsorship opportunity for major marketspace services can benefit from the associations created. However, it should be remembered that, as noted earlier, many of these services, especially the high-value, automated ones, occur invisibly with the result that exposure may be limited to first encounter and any ancillary marketing that is permitted.

IMPLICATIONS FOR TRADITIONAL INDUSTRY CATEGORIES

Finally, let's look briefly at how the above observations translate into opportunities for retailers, manufacturers and financial services.

Retailers

Retailers have tended to view digital markets as a simple extension of the shop window, effectively 'virtual shelf space'. The most obvious symptom of this approach is the prevalence of catalogue-driven applications, which have often suffered badly from trying to leverage earnings from the most price-sensitive end of the transaction. The outcome has been, as it has with so many other comparable efforts, that these initiatives play directly into the now-familiar commoditising tendencies of the Internet with the consequent effects on margin.

A genuine threat for retailers, on the other hand, lies in the real opportunities for producers and wholesalers to reach customers directly and, more subtly, in the increasing use of the market for demand management. Some categories have also seen an increase in demand aggregation services and in some instances provision of direct customer access to business exchanges. All this increases the possibility of disintermediation, of being effectively cut out of the chain.

However, deploying their expert knowledge and their premises can dramatically increase the revenue sources available to retailers and, in respect of delivery and after-sales service, make them a critical, physical (as in bricks-and-mortar) interface with the customer. Significantly, this transformation into experts, brokers and service providers also exploits the strengths of digital channels, while limiting exposure to margin erosion.

KEY POINT

One obvious defence lies in the customer assurance that the brand familiarity of many high street names provides. However, retailers have other strengths that enable them to play highly effective – if unanticipated – roles in marketspaces. Their product and customer knowledge, buying expertise, and sales and delivery services, all place them credibly as potential experts, brokers, and localised service providers.

Manufacturers

As competitive owners of production capacity, manufacturers risk cannibalising their core business if they own or run marketspaces, though the opportunity to invest separately is always open. The more tangible opportunity will lie in using marketspaces to create and sustain direct relationships with end customers. This has two major benefits:

1   Access to lead consumers provides both increased customer information and participation, enabling rapid and responsive product design and earlier market testing.
2   For the increasing number of manufacturers who use modular design-and-build processes, appropriate types of marketspaces can become the 'last leg of operations'. Final configuration and assembly can be performed in conjunction with the customer, who specifies preferences in terms of product configuration and options. The result is a form of personal customisation that both commands a price premium and actively supports the objectives of marketspaces.

Financial services

Some of the greatest success stories in application of the digital media have come from the financial sector, Schwab providing one well-known example, and several on-line banking systems have enjoyed some success. In theory the nature of their relationship with customers makes financial services perfectly positioned to own and control marketspaces. As providers of services of high consumer concern in long-term relationship with their clients, financial services should be able to provide the kind of high-trust environment that is demanded.

But in practice, apart from some early and unimaginative forays into badging of online shopping mall concepts, many financial services have restricted themselves to using digital media in pursuit of two opportunities:

1   The reduction of operational costs through providing customer interfaces and transaction services online. Reduction in operational cost is a competitive imperative, once some players have taken the first steps, but strategies based on endless improvements to operational efficiency and economies of scale reach a logical point of diminishing returns. (And the consequent 'impersonalisation' of the customer interface may also cause collateral damage to the trust relationship). While this is a necessary component of strategy, it fails to take advantage of the opportunities that digital markets offer, and unless balanced with initiatives to counter any damage to the relationship, can actually reduce future options.

2   The cross-selling of commoditised products, which, unless these are all genuinely 'best value for money', in any transparent marketplace destroys the essential trust relationship in favour of elusive incremental sales.

There continues to be an urgent need for honest brokers in financial services who offer not only impartial advice about a full range of offers from all major players, but also provide appropriate windows of access into the wholesale markets. But with some notable exceptions, traditional financial services have not risen to the challenge. Instead new players are emerging who are willing to confront the issue, especially through direct or brokered access to the wholesale market for wealthy individuals (and there is a decreasing net worth entry barrier). Such services allow customers to tailor portfolios and insurance instruments to their own needs, rather than select the best fit from a limited range. Provided they accompany these services with information and learning for the customer, and the ability to reduce or spread risks, this new breed of player is likely to capture much of the value potentially available to financial services in marketspaces.

This is not to suggest that banking customers do not still need dedicated, digital, account-management services, only that other services are best sold through marketspace configurations, where proprietary products are not the primary *raison d'être*.

TO SUMMARISE

- Information of value to a marketspace is possessed by a wide range of organisations, who can benefit directly because it becomes possible to create revenue by charging for the use of the core product rather than having to aggregate huge quantities in order to sell advertising space.
- Directories find a natural requirement for their services throughout marketspaces, and are enabled to extend their business model to include a range of service and certification features that create opportunities for new revenue streams.
- Experts, learning providers and brokers are enfranchised, being able to offer their services as a direct input into the customer's task set, when choices they can support are being made. Their consultancy and advice is critical to both owners and customers, engendering a range of opportunities.
- Differentiated products and services are the direct beneficiaries of the return of value created when real needs meet with expert advice and structured selection techniques. For them the relentless commoditisation of transparent markets is reversed.
- Advertisers have fewer opportunities to engage: the structured nature of the material makes marketing messages intrusive, but sponsorship offers a potentially valuable substitute.
- For retailers, the opportunity to leverage their knowledge, services and systems within a marketspace may interestingly be greater than earning a margin on sales.

- Manufacturers can use marketspaces to improve product development by working directly with lead users, and to customise their products in collaboration with customers.
- Financial services have immense opportunities, but established players require a change of outlook before they can comfortably take advantage of them.

NOTES

1   A choice-board is any component of the interface that structures the selection of optional components of a purchase (e.g. the customer purchasing a car will need a structured way to choose from the range of colours, trims, wheels etc. that are available and be able to visualise the result of their choices).

2   An information asymmetry exists when one party has access to information that is unavailable to the other.

CHAPTER 10

Rules and Relationships in Marketspaces

... Alice soon came to the conclusion that it was a very difficult game indeed. The players all played at once, without waiting for turns, quarrelling all the while, and fighting for the hedgehogs; and in a very short time the Queen was in a furious passion, and went stamping about, and shouting 'Off with his head!' or 'Off with her head' about once in a minute.

IN THIS CHAPTER WE LOOK AT

- management issues that are unique to digital businesses and marketspaces in particular;
- the critical role of the central management or owners;
- the concerns of customer perception and experience;
- balancing the tensions among key partners and allies;
- deriving the strategic benefits of the marketspace configuration; and
- sustainability of marketspace strategies.

THE IMPORTANCE OF MARKETSPACE OWNERS

We concern ourselves initially with the role, the challenges and the benefits of marketspace ownership and management. Isolating the distinctive management issues, we summarise the major components and look at the establishment of identity, support of trust, management of accessibility, the creation of the infrastructure and taking responsibility for the relationship dynamics. We conclude the chapter with a discussion of the benefits of the marketspace configuration to the profitability and sustainability of a digital business.

Whether a marketspace is primarily owned by a single business or run as a partnership, the role of the management is critical to the maintenance of its identity and focus, the management of customer perception and the balance and relationships of the component parts. Unless participant businesses or departments are willing to relinquish these roles to an overriding management structure, the marketspace has little chance of optimising the benefits for all its members. Attempts to control these variables through ad hoc negotiation are almost certain to founder on the distinctive perceptions and, ultimately, the self-interest of the individual members.

MANAGEMENT ISSUES THAT ARE DISTINCTIVE TO MARKETSPACES

It is not the intention of this chapter to explore all the management issues in detail (many of them are the generic concerns of all businesses) rather we focus on the critical concerns that are particular to, or of critical importance within, the marketspace configuration. We have made the assumption that management will take responsibility for optimising return on investment and shareholder value or, in the case of not-for-profit operations, fulfilment of the mandate, according to the imperatives of the particular business. We will not therefore adopt this perspective as an explicit framework, although many of the issues we explore will influence how that is to be achieved.

To help us to distinguish issues that are critical to marketspaces and their management, we approach the management concerns as if they were independent of ownership of most of the components. Thus, purely for the sake of clarity, the assumption will be made that partner companies supply all the information, expertise and products and services that are required. The management is then responsible for infrastructure, provision of support for transactions, communication and collaboration and all automated services, which, representing as they do the critical customer 'lock-in' and the 'invisible' component of the brand, are issues of core competence. This allows us to concentrate attention on the capabilities required to leverage the components of the marketspace into a sustainable, competitive business, optimising the benefit for all.

What then are the distinctive issues? To answer that we will return to our 'Cycles of Customer Experience' diagram, illustrating the interaction between the customer's state of engagement and the state of their perception and commitment to the service (Fig. 10.1).

Using this we can identify a category of key management roles associated with the interlocking cycles and explore three major sets of tasks. The first, *management of customer perception,* concerns the outer cycle, and includes the establishment and identity of the marketspace. Under this heading we can discern three critical tasks:

- managing identity and perception;
- management of the framework for trust; and
- fostering the perception of value and commitment.

A second major set of tasks concerns the inner cycle, and we'll

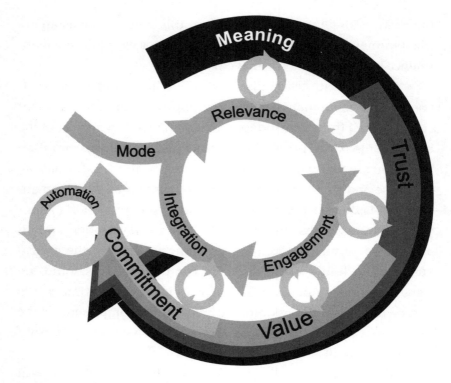

Fig. 10.1 The Cycles of Customer Experience tool revisited.

call it *management of customer engagement*. Bearing in mind our assumption for the sake of this analysis that, with the exception of automated services, partners supply all the components of the marketspace and that therefore the customer is transacting with third parties, this consists in:

- analysing and maintaining the modal framework;
- providing and maintaining marketspace infrastructure; and
- managing automated service provision.

Finally, in respect of tasks associated with the interplay of the two cycles, we can conceive trustpoints as the lubricant that move the customer from perception to action and back. The task here is the identification and *management of the trustpoint requirements.*

A second category of critical management tasks, *managing the value network,* concerning the management of customer and partner relationships and external alliances, will depend in part on marketspace composition. Again, for the purpose of clarity, we will assume the partnership structure outlined at the start of this section.

Lastly, some issues concerning fully *exploiting the benefits* of the marketspace configuration through optimising marketing scope and fostering customer commitment, are a question of the dynamics, and we will take a brief look at these towards the end of this chapter.

HARD HAT AREA!

A CLOSER LOOK AT THE DISTINCTIVE CONCERNS

We now investigate the management tasks identified in more detail. Once again many of the components will prove to consist largely of generic management skills, and we will only provide comment on those elements that are specific to digital markets, and to marketspaces in particular.

Management of customer perception

We identified the three principal components of this task as:

- managing identity and perception;
- management of the framework for trust; and
- fostering the perception of value and commitment.

Let's now take each of these in turn.

Managing identity and perception

This includes:

- establishing and clarifying the *domain or domains of customer concern* that are to be addressed;
- specifying the focus by *setting and policing clear boundaries* to ensure that customers are not confused and frustrated;
- creating the *marketspace value proposition, brand positioning and differentiation* from others with similar domain coverage; and
- *managing accessibility* by ensuring that the service is available through all appropriate channels as and when customer purpose creates the need for it.

The first three elements together address the value proposition and answer the questions:

- Who is this service for?
- What is its scope and where are the boundaries?
- How is it delivered?

To address these issues management must establish key features.

Domain and focus

As we have explored elsewhere, marketspaces exist within one or more domains or realms of customer interest, in that they fall under particular topics or areas of concern. To take a fresh example, a putative marketspace concerning classical music would occupy a broad consumer domain called 'leisure' and also one called 'culture'. For employees of the industry and performers, it might lives primarily in the domain of work. Classical music is also a focused subset of a larger potential marketspace for music, and contains subsets of its own such as Baroque music (Fig. 10.2).

The owners need to make strategic decisions as to which domains the marketspace will cater to, and where its boundaries

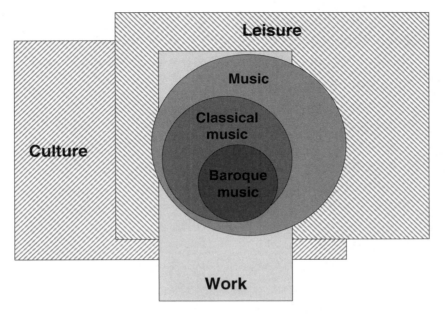

Fig. 10.2 Domains and boundaries for a classical music marketspace.

will lie within each. A larger marketspace with a broad focus on 'music' might not be able to cater fully for all the subsets of musical interest it contains. Indeed in necessarily providing a great deal of information that lovers of classical music will find irrelevant, it might be subject to what we call 'hollowing out', once the perceived value moves from product sales to in-depth provision of services.

This highlights an acute competitive issue. In general the balance between a broad 'space' encompassing high customer numbers, and a narrower space providing higher value to fewer customers will be critical. In an environment where viability is decided by our promiscuous customer, the quality and completeness of the service is so important, that overly broad 'spaces' will be subject to rapid 'hollowing out' by better targeted offers. On the other hand many potential marketspaces may be just too small to support a viable business.

ESTABLISHING FOCUS AND BOUNDARIES

A number of questions about the proposal need to be addressed at the outset:

1 Which primary domain is the marketspace intending to address?
2 Is there a clear central proposition addressing identifiable customer concerns?
3 Are those concerns sufficiently distinct from the general concerns of a larger grouping (e.g. classical music as a subset of music)?
4 Within the primary domain, is it possible to define the boundaries of the marketspace, or is what is not included ill-defined?
5 Do the interests of potential users from other domains intersect with those in the primary one in such a way as to create synergies by catering for both, as may be the case with childcare specialists and parents? Or are their concerns so different that they must be addressed through different services?
6 Are its subsets themselves so identifiable and focused that users whose concern is that subset would rather have a devoted service?

Once the focus is clear, the establishment and maintenance of rational boundaries is a necessity, and not just for brand identity; failure to do so risks destroying clarity of meaning, and with it trust. Once established, these boundaries create a governing logic by which rules that exclude information, goods and services that are not core to the proposition, can be formulated and enforced.

Brand and differentiation

On the Commoditised Internet, the challenges of brand management have, in almost all cases, been approached with an essentially off-line mentality. Brand development has revolved primarily around the concerns of marketing and profile and, while certain alliances have raised issues of brand identity and hierarchy (for example where a specialised content owner joins partners with a portal), the work has in general resided with marketers and corporate identity designers. This is inadequate to the need, a detailed focus on customers' experience as they tackle individual tasks is required.

KEY POINT

As we have stressed in 'Mode, Purpose and Task', beyond the issues of focus and identity, it is essential to accept that the customer experience of the service will to a large degree define their understanding of the brand. Modal analysis has a critical role to play here.

Many other brand considerations will depend on the specifics of marketspace composition. Typically though, the very necessary range, diversity and complexity of the partnerships and alliances required to create a satisfactory marketspace will give rise to conflicts of identity and strategic intent whose resolution is by no means adequately achieved through brand strategy alone. However, it will be a critical role of owners to take on, and flexibly manage the clear and powerful expression through brand communications of the marketspace's identity and values. In the context of this imperative, the need for diplomatic yet firm public control of a plethora of participating brands – each with its own agenda, many in theoretical conflict with each other – will be a tough and critical role for owners.

A number of other levers are available to help the owners establish the characteristics of the marketspace that distinguish it from other potentially similar offers with which it may compete. As well as differences of focus this will include the espoused values, the selection and identity of components, the range and nature of customer touchpoints for access and the geographic and demographic scope.

The management of access

As we have discussed throughout, the provision and balancing

THE CHOICE OF POSITIONING

Mission and values

Placing the customer at the heart of the strategy provides the opportunity for the owners of different marketspaces to select from a range of possible missions and to stand for a set of values with which customers can identify. Thus one business might approach the childcare market from the standpoint of maximising convenience for working parents; another might concentrate on reassurance, advice and problem sharing. Many of the core resources and offers would be similar, indeed the full set of services might appear a close match, but the strategic intent and the target customer would be different.

Configuration, completeness and scope

Further differentiation between potential realisations of a marketspace is evident in the choice of participants, their capabilities, the integration of their services and the overall fit that is established. The requirement for perceived completeness, explored later, obliges the owners to ensure an adequate balance and range of products, services and information resources.

Geographical and demographic scope, as well as the boundaries of the service itself, will affect what constitutes completeness within any market.

Customer interface and benefits

The range of opportunities to configure the customer interface and the underlying resources allows great flexibility in defining and delivering targeted customer benefits. For instance, the owners have the opportunity, where it adds value, to provide customers with a transparent window into the supply chain, enabling them to purchase products and services direct. This may serve to further reduce the cost of commodity items or to provide a better and more flexible range of product configurations. The role of a retail intermediary in digital markets is only valid where product complexity, demand consolidation or complexities of fulfilment demand it.

Other opportunities to adjust the customer interface lie in the choice of presentation. Automated services, for instance, may feature as an explicit benefit, or they may be bundled with other products and services.

of multiple channels for access presents a primary challenge for marketspaces' management. Modal analysis provides the raw information, enabling decisions about preferred configuration, which channels must be available, and how they are best deployed. Many channels, however, have limited reach, and the size and profile of their customer base will be a decisive factor in selection.

Good stewardship demands close consideration of a second factor. The owners must balance and manage channels as 'choke points', since the channel owner will often be in a position to capture a part of the economic value in the form of fees, required use of channel owned services, or a margin of the transaction. These issues are addressed in greater detail under *managing the value network*, below.

Management of the framework for trust

This set of tasks concerns the macro issues of trust, in that it provides the essential foundations by which customer trust is fostered, as distinct from the micro concerns of managing trust-points, which we will touch on again later. As we have seen, trust is a complex issue. We have already examined the foundations in the form of security, clarity about the customer relationship and the use of customer data. These establish ground-rules that must be accepted by all players. We have also referred to neutrality, external certification and validation, and the need for responsiveness.

The full range of aspects to a trust relationship is diverse, and will contain elements that are particular to a given marketspace. It is a primary task of the owner to identify all the relevant concerns, make provisions where possible, and provide and police ground-rules for the remainder.

The generic tasks can be identified as:

- establishing and managing the *security and privacy policies and features*;
- identifying and meeting requirements for *third-party certification and validation*;
- ensuring *adequate completeness* of the components in respect of customer purpose and tasks;
- observing the *imperative of neutrality*;
- minimising *perceived dissonance*;
- *policing internal marketing and the use of customer data*.

Many of these concerns, such as the security and privacy requirements and the need for external certification, are either well known or have been adequately explored in earlier chapters. However, the issues of completeness and neutrality, as well as the newly introduced concept of dissonance, bear further discussion.

The requirement for 'bounded completeness' and neutrality

Marketspaces have two completeness requirements. The first concerns ensuring that, as far as possible, all resources required to meet the identified customer purposes and task sets are available within the marketspace. The second is the related requirement for perceived independence and neutrality.

Since in digital markets consumers can, directly or with the assistance of intelligent agents, access the details and prices of the full range of any product or service they require, forcing them to work for that information is a denial of trust. Services organised on marketspace principles therefore need to ensure that customers have rapid access to a range of offers that is at least representative, and ideally comprehensive.

KEY POINT

Trust, as we have seen, is hard to establish and easy to destroy. Perceived bias, especially in the selection of products and services that are made available, is one quick way to destroy it. Taken together, completeness and neutrality make it hard for producers to play an ownership role in marketspaces.

Minimising perceived dissonance

The transparency of the digital environment ensures that customers quickly become aware, either through their own browsing or through peers, of inconsistencies in the messages, prices and communications activities of service providers. This extends, with the potential for greater long-term damage, to discrepancies between the espoused values of the organisation and its actual behaviour. Fig. 10.3 captures some of the major potential conflicts.

In a marketspace, the problem is exacerbated by the many participating partners and suppliers. We have already touched on the brand conflicts that may arise, but both far subtler behaviours in the everyday contact, and the activities of participants outside the marketspace arena, have the potential for undermining trust. The selection of partners and the rules of engagement both need to be rigorous if trust is to be preserved.

Fostering the perception of value and commitment

Getting customers to perceive meaning and relevance in the offer, and establishing a trust relationship, are only the precursors to the all-important commercial relationship. A viable business needs customers to purchase and keep purchasing. This will not happen if they do not perceive value in the goods and services, or if

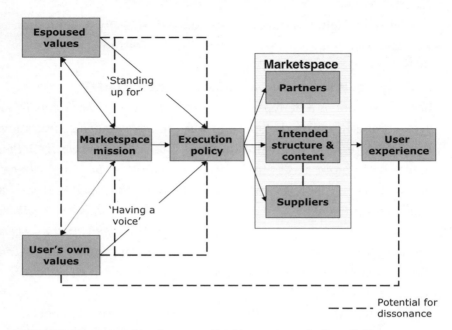

Fig. 10.3 The potential for dissonance. Solid lines indicate the flow of influences, dashed lines the major potential discrepancies between expectation and realisation.

the buying experience or after-sales follow-through is unsatisfactory. Careful attention is essential, bearing in mind that the ideal outcome is for customers to entrust the service with the automatic handling of major tasks. We identify five primary responsibilities:

- guaranteeing that all products and services include *competitively priced* options as well as any differentiated or luxury variants;
- designing and managing a usable, reliable and quick *buying experience*;
- agreeing and regulating *response and fulfilment* targets for all transactions;
- identifying opportunities to simplify and *automate the customers' task set*; and

- extending trust and transaction support into any desirable *secondary peer-to-peer markets*.

These are all influences on customer perception that can, to a limited degree, be controlled. Once again the majority of them are largely self-explanatory. Competitive pricing, especially for commodity items, is a *sine qua non* of digital trading, unsatisfactory buying experiences are the major reason why customers abort digital transactions, and the post-sales experience is at least as critical. The wise marketspace owner will underwrite and guarantee all transactions conducted through the service.

Automation has been examined in some detail earlier, but clearly the initial analytical approach to identifying opportunities will need to be augmented by customer research and extensive trials, if maximum benefit is to be derived by business and customer.

Services for the peer-to-peer market

Extending services into the peer-to-peer market may seem out of place. In fact this is the ideal opportunity to become a touchstone of value for the customer. The simple provision of expert advice and access to a secure transaction mechanic through a trusted provider, can build the customer relationship more soundly then any amount of direct communications can achieve.

As this is primarily a relationship management issue, we address it and its benefits in more detail in *Managing the Value Network* below.

Management of customer engagement

The second major set of tasks associated with customer experience is connected with the inner, engagement ring of the Cycles of Customer Experience tool. Unlike the foregoing, this is about the minutiae of the experience, ensuring that provision is as easy to understand and use as is possible, and about building robust systems. We identified three components:

- analysing and maintaining the modal framework;
- providing and maintaining marketspace infrastructure; and
- managing automated service provision.

Analysing and maintaining the modal framework

Examining this in more detail, it consists of four tasks:

- understanding the full range of *customers' modes of interaction and purposes* and analysing the appropriate responses and task sets;
- providing easy access on arrival to *relevant, and where possible complete, task solutions* to meet all identified customer purposes;
- seeking opportunities to address as full *a range of customer concerns* in respect of the domain as is economically viable; and
- *distinguishing, locating and configuring the components* necessary to deliver the full range of information, expertise, certification and products and services required.

All have already been explored in Chapter 4, 'Modes, Purposes and Tasks', and Chapter 7, 'The Marketspace'.

Providing and maintaining marketspace infrastructure

These activities are concerned with building, or procuring and managing, the key assets and capabilities of the service infrastructure and include:

- building and managing the *transaction, communication and collaboration infrastructure*; and
- establishing, maintaining (and ensuring the confidentiality of) all *customer profiles and data*.

After the initial design and build of the marketspace, these tasks, for the most part, reduce to a series of issues about core competence, capabilities and processes.

Creation of capabilities and processes

As usual, core processes will depend on strategic objectives, the value proposition and the combination of skills required for delivering on them.

In any marketspace, the backbone of essential core services provided by the management will include:

- automated and semi-automated services;
- core transaction services;
- customer communication and collaboration services;
- trust and authentication services;
- one or more directories; and
- infrastructure and rules for business process integration.

Many other services will be specific to the individual marketspace. Core processes will be needed to handle all of these 'owner-provided' components, and to deal with customer support and feedback.

A core competence in recognising and responding to customer modes and purposes is of course essential in a marketspace, but not the sum total of distinctive capabilities that are required. On the contrary, core competencies to deliver on the value proposition will vary greatly, partly in reflection of the revenue model. Different strategic objectives for innovation or improved operational effectiveness will define which competencies create the possibility of excellence.

Managing automated service provision

Two largely self-explanatory tasks follow from the use of modal analysis to simplify and automate customer task sets:

- ensuring the availability of all necessary data feeds for *maintenance or triggering of automated services*; and
- providing secure and reliable *management of automated services*.

Managing the trustpoint requirement

We have been describing trustpoints as the lubricant that moves customers from perception to action and back. This is an oversimplification, as many trustpoint requirements are connected with authentication of material or simple respect for human behavioural preferences, but it is a useful way of thinking about the management issues.

Identifying trustpoints is a task that we described in more detail in Chapter 7, 'The Marketspace', and is a final stage of the modal analysis process. The management task is simply stated, but complex in performance: identify all trustpoint needs and devise the simplest, most thorough satisfaction achievable. This will often involve research, and the market testing of alternatives.

MANAGING THE VALUE NETWORK

This category of management concerns covers a range of relationship issues: we will focus on those with customers and with marketspace members and alliance partners. Many relationship-building and guardianship tasks, such as primary marketing, are generic management issues, but challenges falling under this broad umbrella that are distinctive to marketspaces include:

- maintaining the *dynamics of the relationship with customers*;
- supporting the *peer-to-peer network*;
- managing the *balance and relationship of service partners and the appropriation of revenue*;
- establishing and managing *alliances with complimentary key services* in adjacent domains; and

- *managing channel relationships* and the relative capture of economic value.

We will address some of these issues in more detail.

Customer relationship dynamics

A key part of a sustainable strategy for marketspace growth lies in the ability to create valuable services that 'lock' the customer in. Getting to this point involves a thoroughly developed engagement strategy. It's obvious by now that reliability and responsiveness are critical; customers are not going to entrust important chores to an unreliable or slow service provider. Any marketspace development strategy must have a plan to cultivate the customer relationship through the provision of timely expert advice and learning, and consistent support for customer purposes that take time to accomplish.

The brand new challenge of peer-to-peer networks

The significance of these new networks has been alluded to above; it is an essential insight for the marketspace owner that ongoing direct interaction between customers requires close attention. Of course, the issue may appear to have been addressed through the provision of communication and collaboration services, but in future digital markets it goes far beyond such threshold provision.

Consumers have always traded with each other of course but, apart from the second-hand car market, and some well-developed collectors' markets such as that for stamps, this has traditionally been a fairly ad hoc business with few enablers and a resolutely 'caveat emptor' outlook. On-line auctions such as eBay started to change this, and the advent of 'pure' peer-to-peer trading systems such as Napster and Gnutella, have helped the market along in this radical and often controversial direction.

For this type of customer trading to truly flourish, however, (and echoing our points made earlier in 'Key Drivers and Enablers of Marketspaces' and above) it needs the support that marketspaces are well positioned to provide: directory systems, expert advice, trust services and transaction mechanics; potentially including auctions, exchanges and file trading. Attention to the needs of the peer market may also reveal a need to extend service provision to the handling of micro-payments and the availability of delivery services. Such an infrastructure will be critical to the dynamic of the market, whether the goods concerned are primarily physical or digital.

It's important to grasp that these developments do not solely benefit customers; they offer marketspace partners many opportunities, arising from a change in perspective on the value chain and increased customer insight.

The extended value chain

In traditional markets the consumer is for the most part treated as the end point of the value chain. In this model, lack of customer visibility up the supply chain creates information asymmetries[1] allowing price differentials between equivalent products to flourish. In fact the asymmetries have always existed both ways: the marketer has equally been denied visibility of the post-sales and secondary markets.

The greater transparency of digital markets has changed that, with the initial outcome, as we have seen, that price transparency in the Commoditised Internet continuously erodes margins. A further change is underway. Whereas the marketer traditionally had limited ability to obtain access to, or real visibility of, customer trading and secondary markets, this access now becomes available. It can provide significant customer, product and market information, as well as onward sales and support opportunities.

Peer-to-peer trading is inherently less structured than business-to-business systems, but the value chain no longer stops

PEER-TO-PEER INVOLVEMENT BENEFITS INFORMATION AND INSIGHT

Marketspace propositions are founded on customer insight, and they evolve over time as customer information and feedback fuel fresh insight. The strategic deployment and analysis of customer information, and its appropriate sharing among partners and suppliers, will dictate direction, speed of growth, and the ability of all components to optimise their delivery and alignment in service of the value proposition, and their own dependent strategies. Engagement with the peer-to-peer market greatly enhances the quantity and quality of the information available.

From the competitive standpoint, good strategic deployment of customer insight will allow first movers to retain an advantage (and of course challengers to catch-up!).

with the principal buyer, and therefore, at least in the appropriate domains, marketspaces can realise whole new types of value for all participants.

Balance and relationship of service partners

Patterns in partnership

Partnerships and alliances of all kinds have been a feature of digital projects from the outset. Whether they are for the creation of infrastructure or for traffic generation, marketing or fulfilment, such associations are understood to be critical, but they are often very loose, and many players still want to manage sales and distribution from sites that they own and control.

In this light, digital services are still being seen as virtual counterparts of existing structural elements of the business, and partnerships as a marriage of independents, not of co-dependents. With the result that many, if not most, participants have been subject to the destructive power of the Commoditised Internet.

The fallacy of total disintermediation

Alliances have been changing subtly anyway. Increasingly, at the time of writing, companies make their Internet sales from microsites, or through service offers embedded within portals or other companies' services. A single player may be more or less deeply engaged with scores of others. But the conscious realisation that, for many participants, there may be no need for a separate, branded presence, has been slow to surface.

Of course some manufacturers allow their products to be displayed on many sites, and most view the digital environment as just another channel to market. But the temptation to attempt to duplicate off-line models on-line, or to circumvent distributors altogether, is both strong and wrong. As we've noted above more than once, both direct sales services and distribution channels that imitate retail models, immediately lay products open to the pressures of transparency and commoditisation that destroy value.

KEY POINT

The new question for most participating businesses in the context of marketspaces needs to be not, 'how can I get maximum exposure?' (the old traffic/footfall-based concept) but 'how can I appear optimally in a value-supporting context?' For producers of goods and services, the answer will increasingly be not 'by featuring in an on-line equivalent to the retailer' but 'by appearing in the appropriate, relevant, high-value information contexts'.

The critical role of relationship management for participants

Whether one company wholly owns the service, or its ownership is shared amongst its participants, there will always be a need to accommodate independent players in a number of expert and product supply roles. Managing this network of partner relationships will be a core competence for marketspace owners. The nature of the relationships will vary, but three significantly differ-

EXPLORING KEY RELATIONSHIPS

Coalition members

We have said that the complex mix of information, products, knowledge, expertise, customer insight and technology that any marketspace will require, is not likely to be available within, or quickly built by, any one organisation, so joint ventures will play a strong role. The members of any joint venture 'coalition' will have a stronger influence on outcomes than other components, and their relative contribution, influence and degree of ownership will define many characteristics of the organisation.

Delivery partners

Beyond the immediate coalition, a range of more or less close partnerships are required to deliver other products and services, expertise or core infrastructure. The greater the significance of their contribution, and the more complete the integration required to deliver customer benefits effectively, the more influence they will exert. Often expert partners will be providing the independent advice that forms a critical element of trust, maintaining an appropriate relationship with them, and between them and product and service providers, will prove challenging if their independence is to be credible.

Product suppliers

Despite generally maintaining a 'supplier' relationship with the marketspace, most product marketers will ultimately interface directly with the customer during the sales or fulfilment process. Indeed, interposing the marketspace as an intermediary may create usability issues, and in some cases an unacceptable price premium. This direct interface means that supplier selection, how they 'fit', their compliance with marketspace rules and their presentation may be critical to success.

ent forms can be distinguished and each needs careful provision. These are:

- coalition members who participate in ownership of the service;
- delivery partners who are key contributors but not owners (experts will commonly appear in this role because of their need to retain independence); and
- product suppliers who provide and deliver the range of products and services.

Key relationship management issues
Two relationship management issues are central.

Internal neutrality and boundary management
Maintenance of customer perception and apportionment of the benefits, oblige the owners to preserve a careful and neutral balance between information, expertise and product providers, to ensure that dominant players are not permitted to displace important but less powerful providers, compromise trust or distort the external boundaries of the marketspace.

The relative power of the members of any ownership coalition, its partners and supplier companies and the boundaries between them, will define the composition, partnership dynamics, and to a substantial degree the customer experience, of any marketspace. Relatively small boundary changes could have profound effects on the relative leverage of the various contributors, and on the 'meaning' and messages perceived by the customer. Internal boundary management is therefore a critical strategic issue.

Partnership dynamics
The possible number of players, and the variety of their strategic ambitions, creates the potential for severe tensions, which can only be managed by the owners.

For example, this is illustrated by the tensions between information publishers, who naturally wish to increase their presence and influence by extending the breadth of coverage, and brokers who come into their own with increasing vertical depth. A third dimension, the option for sector or international market extension, further complicates the picture. Each party may favour such a move if it aligns with its own current reach or planned expansion, but not otherwise. We use a simple graphical method for plotting such tensions by mapping their major dimensions as illustrated in Fig. 10.4.

Alliances with complementary key services

Ensuring that suitable agreements for mutual presence and referral exist with complementary service providers will be critical for two reasons.

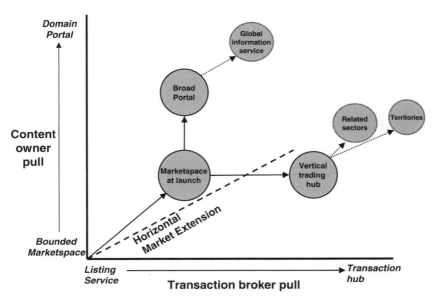

Fig. 10.4 One way of mapping marketspace tensions: content owners will wish to see more of their material featured and pull the service towards an information-rich environment. Brokers on the other hand will wish to extend transaction services. Each will have different expansion ambitions.

1   Cross promotion through referral of traffic is a well-established marketing tool in digital business, and benefits both parties;

2   Less obviously, the boundaries of marketspace domain coverage are to a large degree arbitrary. Despite efforts to establish natural limits to the breadth of the offer, some customers will always need access to related services that lie outside its umbrella. This access needs to be enabled, and managers will seek to identify and affiliate with appropriate allies.

Channels and their integration

We referred above to the management of access and the need to ensure appropriate channel availability, but the issue also has critical importance for the capture of economic value. Once digital presence is extended beyond a dial-up interface with the Internet to always-on mobile channels or to interactive television, the structural relationships change. The service can no longer be made available solely by providing an Internet site for customers to access. Several channels are usually required, and these act as intermediaries between the marketspace and the customer. The marketspace owner will pay for more than just technology to ensure that customers have useful and convenient access. Mobile and television channels are not public networks subject to regulatory supervision of access. They have private owners who act as 'choke points', being in a position – indeed in many cases specifically in business – to levy charges for the use of their infrastructure, and of course access to their customer base.

KEY POINT

Fortunately channel owners, despite many attempts to go it alone, are as dependent on being able to offer a full range of services as these services are on access to their customers. Thus the relationship is symbiotic in nature, and its balance will depend on the market reach the channel provides in comparison with the value the service brings to the channel for customer acquisition or retention.

CHANNEL MANAGEMENT ISSUES

The scope for channel owners to extract economic value from transactions carried out on their service, varies according to the attributes and core revenue model of the channel concerned, as well as the general structure of the industry. Fixed-link, dial-up networks permit the network owner only to levy line-rental charges; hosting and transaction services are independent and carriers share common protocols and universal connectivity. This is not true of mobile channels or of television access; in both cases, proprietary technology and protocols, and restrictions of supplier access, apply. In effect therefore, services may only be able to appear on such channels by permission of the owners, and lack of universal connectivity means that even being granted access is no guarantee of connection or exposure to the majority of the marketspace's customer base.

Furthermore, many channels are likely to wish – or even require – services to use the channel's billing facilities for transactions taking place while customers use the channel.

These challenges mean that:

- In order to reserve their negotiating position, owners must ensure that universal free or line-cost access is available wherever possible.
- Once the balance of channels required is ascertained, their selection becomes a matter of customer demographics, often purely a measure of the percentage of the critical audience that each channel can reach, as much as cost minimisation, restricting negotiating power. Channels with good coverage of the primary customer base will be in a commanding position.

From the point of view of the customer, the desirability or otherwise of a marketspace may be as strongly influenced by the balance of channels, as by its composition and marketing. From the owner's perspective, relationships with channel owners may affect economic viability.

EXPLOITING THE BENEFITS

Beyond the issues raised in connection with customer perception and experience, and the complexities of the network of relationships, managers will work to take advantage of the key benefits to profitability and sustainable advantage offered by the marketspace model. Some of these are explored below.

Capture of economic value

In owning and controlling the infrastructure, definition and boundaries of the marketspace, owners are themselves a 'choke point' controlling access to the customer. All other participants will pay in some way for this access, to a degree that will tend to depend on their leverage.

As we have pointed out, a marketspace is in turn subject to some capture of economic value by channel owners where mobile or iTV channels are required outlets. However, a powerful value proposition and the strong potential for customer commitment over time, arm the marketspace with substantial leverage.

Sustainability of the competitive strategy

Competitor 'lock-out'

The customer lock-in that arises from full service, continuous access, and especially from automation, offers a substantial opportunity for competitor 'lock-out'. Learning from early feedback, and application of the knowledge gained to improving customer understanding and customer benefits, reinforces any early lead. A positive feedback loop is in operation. However, first movers will often be groping their way slowly towards an optimum configuration and fast followers may have an excellent opportunity to take advantage of their learning.

Barriers to imitation

The distinctive meaning created within the marketspace, the breadth of its focus, and the specific configuration of resources that are deployed to deliver and support it, create a unique set of customer benefits. The strategic flexibility of the marketspace model, the mix of partners and the balance of leverage among them, equally ensure that no two propositions will appear identical to the customer. The sources of advantage will necessarily be 'opaque', making successful marketspaces hard to imitate. However, as noted above, they may be subject to encroachment from adjacent markets, hollowing out by more focused models, or engulfment by broader ones.

Focus

Focus is inherent in the marketspace proposition. By providing a more or less coherent mixture of products and services, whose unifying principle is the satisfaction of a particular set of related customer needs, a marketspace is founded on real customer focus, and lives or dies by its ability to capture and exploit customer knowledge. This clarity of the value proposition is the foundation of the marketing advantages outlined below, and promotes efficiency of asset use, ensuring that investment is directed only at those aspects of the service that create well-defined customer benefits.

Marketing scope

Much of the marketing is likely to take place in collaboration with partners and allies, through co-marketing, specialised media and PR. Money saved on mass-media communications can therefore be spent on improving conversion and retention, rather than on initial attraction, thus reinforcing learning and customer lock-in.

SOURCES OF BENEFIT TO MARKETING SCOPE

Network effects

The interaction of the community and wider peer-group membership, augmented by communication and collaboration systems, ensures that existing users attract new ones. The scale of this effect will vary depending on the nature of the marketspace (for example, the domains of concern covered, the specific focus and the consequent scope for collaboration) and on the task sets supported (some lead more naturally to wider participative activities than others do). In the extreme case, viral marketing or peer-group networking become self-sustaining sales mechanics, where information flows between peers are more powerful than any marketing campaign.

Scope economies

Economies of scope through co-marketing with partners support the interest of all participants. Limited marketing collateral can serve multiple uses, and the piggyback effect of riding on other marketing campaigns serves to amplify its effectiveness. The overall effect again is to lower the cost of initial, attraction marketing and reinforce the emphasis on conversion and retention.

Focus on conversion and retention

As the foregoing implies, conversion and retention are central to and supported by the marketspace configuration. With its focus on recognising and supporting customers' modes and the task sets that fulfil their purpose, the marketspace has these objectives at the heart of its proposition, not merely as an accident of 'product fit' and discretionary progression to further purchase.

REDUCING THE RISKS TO SUSTAINABILITY

Focus strategies run the risk that customer preference and behaviour change, leaving the focused service provider with a devalued proposition and a declining market. Permanently locking the market boundaries, composition, delivery configuration and customer relationship dynamics, risks inflexibility if social or economic trends move against it.

For longer-term planning, insight into broader social trends and potentially disruptive technologies and business models will be needed. The multiple owners and contributors can be an asset here, bringing different perspectives and insights, but collection and analysis of this information will, of course, need co-ordination if any effective early detection is to be achieved.

KEY POINT

Judiciously employed, the customer information and insight available within a marketspace will enable early detection of market changes, and the multiple partners and components of its structure assist rapid reconfiguration to respond to them. Such a structure is inherently dynamic and responsive. Moreover the spreading of investment between partners can reduce the capital outlay for each, creating the potential for lower and earlier breakeven, and therefore less lock-in to the objectives of an original business plan.

TO SUMMARISE

- Marketspaces create many distinctive management challenges that require careful addressing if any strategy is to work.

- One central role is the management of customer perception, including identity and focus, the framework for trust and the perceived value of the offer.
- Another lies in managing the customer experience through the use of modal analysis, and providing the infrastructure through which it is realised.
- Owners must also manage the minutiae of trustpoints, if the customer is to translate positive perception into active engagement.
- Management of customer relationships challenges the owners to extend the provision of services for activities that occur outside the boundaries of the system, and rewards them with invaluable customer information and new opportunities.
- Relationships within the marketspace between partners demand the creation of a rule-based framework, and careful balancing of the multiplicity of interests and brands.
- Channel owners are critical 'choke points', capturing economic value by levying charges for customer access and use of their services: their selection and the terms of engagement affect profitability as well as customer perception.
- The marketspace configuration offers multiple sources of sustainable competitive advantage and marketing scope. To benefit, owners will need to effectively manage these benefits on behalf of the diverse interests of all participants.

NOTES

1   An information asymmetry exists when one party has access to information that is unavailable to the other.

CHAPTER II

The Return of Value to Digital Markets

'Everything's got a moral, if you can just find it.'

IN THIS CHAPTER WE LOOK AT

- how changes to access characteristics create and interact with changes to the organisation of information;
- which combinations of access and information are likely to furnish valuable services;
- how portals and marketspaces are positioned to deliver these services;
- the difference that depth of support for the customer concern makes; and
- a summary of the strategic contentions and conclusions of this book.

A PAUSE BEFORE THE LAST STRETCH

As our argument has extended through this book, you will have probably noted three key recurring themes:

- How can *information be organised* in digital markets to optimise support for customer purpose by fostering meaning and trust? (See: 'What's Wrong with the Internet?' and 'Meaning, Trust and Value'.)
- How can *device and channel strategies* be combined to offer customers the best possible access, according to their unique current mode? (See: 'What's Wrong with the Internet?' and 'Modes, Purposes and Tasks'.)
- How can the *depth of support* for customer purpose in a particular domain be maximised? (See: 'What's Wrong with the Internet?' and 'Modes, Purposes and Tasks'.)

We've proposed our own discipline of Modal Analysis as offering the best toolkit for unpacking and answering these questions, with the three elements of mode – environmental, contextual and purposive – enabling management to 'triangulate' on our key themes above, and to identify how to provide most value to the desirable customer in tomorrow's digital marketplace.

In the heart of the book (Chapters 7–10) we've examined how this proposed solution plays out for both customers and the full range of key business types, using our new paradigm for value, the marketspace.

In this last chapter, we will apply those three concerns, the organisation of information, depth of support and extent of accessibility, to create a concluding framework, visualised as our 'Value Cube' tool.

This approach enables us to locate precisely where future value lies for our promiscuous customer, and thus where our invisible brands need to be most focused.

We conclude the chapter with a brief summary of our strategic contentions, which will help to crystallise what we see as a robust vision of the problems facing business in digital markets at the time of writing, how those problems have come about, and the form that a viable new paradigm for the delivery of value will take.

A CHANGE OF PARADIGM

Revisiting our Revenue Cube from Chapter 3, we see that it is successful in capturing so many current Internet business models because, like them, it focuses exclusively on the products and the mechanics of the transaction. On the Commoditised Internet, aggregation of either audiences or products is a dominant theme; the underlying assumptions are usually that value is added through the reduction of transaction costs, and that overwhelming quantity amply compensates for any shortcomings in quality. Awkward questions about how customers experience this, and whether it really adds value for them, are ignored or brushed aside.

KEY POINT

The marketspace concept offers us the opportunity to change perspective, to approach the problem from the point-of-view of the customer and thus to uncover the new paradigm that is driving value creation. It is time to expose an underlying theme of this book: the Internet, the great disrupter of business, is about to see the businesses it has spawned be themselves disrupted, and not by the technology.

Each new technology and device is recruited to the service of stretching the model, increasing the audience, and extending the range. Like bloated department stores (whose growth and subsequent slow decline may hold lessons for the future) whole departments, floors and branches are added, compelled by the underlying logic.

Transfixed in the headlights of the oncoming rush of technical widgetry, we remain unable to focus on the underlying truth that, as Clayton Christiansen has acutely observed in *The Innova-*

tor's Dilemma[1] and elsewhere – technology is not the only source of disruptive innovation.

WHERE WILL TOMORROW'S VALUE BE FOUND?

The customer experience of the new access attributes

When access is largely through dial-up appliances, service provision is constrained by discontinuities in time and space. When restricted to this dial-up environment, Modal Analysis reveals the shortcomings of a service that can only address very limited task sequences, falling well short of fulfilling the full customer purpose. Typically such services satisfy only partial value chains, and therefore offer only limited customer value. Thus, however good our intention, without service continuity the relentless commoditisation of products and services marketed through the Internet is likely to continue.

The changes that create the real marketspace opportunity are only fully realisable as continuous access over portable devices becomes widely available. To take advantage of such changes, as we shall see, a matching change to the organisation of the underlying material is also needed.

Access characteristics first moved from the original 'Fixed-link' dial-up, to access from anywhere over mobile devices – 'Ubiquitous' – but still requiring dial-up operation. The next stage, 'Selective/Continuous', is arriving with devices that are always-on, and whose target channel is usually selected by the user.

A final step for some services, what we call 'pervasive' access, will be reached when dedicated devices are embedded in products, or worn on the person, and are in continuous contact with one or more services. The distinguishing characteristic of pervasive access is that constant connection with the service is maintained, without the customer needing to select or be aware

SELECTIVE/CONTINUOUS ACCESS

In this mode of operation a customer selects the service to which a mobile device is connected so that it provides continuous support for their current activity. Its interface displays a primary service resource that is thereby instantly available when needed. In our GoKids example, for instance, Christopher might be in continuous contact for support whilst he is in a shopping centre purchasing children's clothes. It could be helping him both to find and to select appropriate items that are hard-wearing and value for money.

Because the device is always on, this channel selection does not preclude the delivery of an important message or request from another, high-priority, service such as notification that tickets for that concert of Baroque music have become available; unless Christopher has blocked such contact. Note that the customer decides on both the primary channel, and which others are permitted to override or break through it.

of it. Trigger information arising from pervasive channels will be one common source of messages and requests that may override, or break through, the chosen channel in selective/continuous mode.

BEHIND THE SCREEN

Wireless technologies are evolving a connectedness that goes far beyond enabling consumers to remain continuously in contact with a supporting service, or making them available for contact at any time; they are becoming embedded in objects with no recognisable interface at all. Speculation about 'smart' refrigerators that can monitor their contents and update the shopping list at the store, or clothes that can monitor the wearer's health, is becoming reality. Everyday appliances and accessories are becoming network nodes that can maintain real-time communication with services, other devices and, of course, customers. And to match these developments, even 'dumb' goods will increasingly carry 'radio tags' that make them recognisable by 'smart' terminals. The network is becoming pervasive, buried in our everyday artefacts.

One outcome is that the capacity to deliver automated services will soon become a threshold characteristic of many products, an expected function, central to the product concept. Another, less obvious one, is a rapid acceleration of the trend towards invisible or minimal contact services, raising resultant issues about their review, management and control. Marketspaces provide a stepping-stone on the way to an appropriate personal service management environment, enabling the assembly of management interfaces within a context that connects with customers' practical and emotional concerns.

Ultimately, just as multiple channels and mobile devices call for a reconfiguration of digital service provision, if value is to be created rather than destroyed, so underlying data flows will need to be restructured to function optimally within the pervasive network. Whatever the mechanics, customers will still need a supportive, trust-engendering environment through which to tap into and interact with these streams, and this environment can only evolve out of collaborative ecosystems equivalent to those provided by marketspaces.

Figure 11.1 illustrates this progression of developments in access.

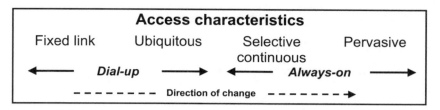

Fig. 11.1 Changing characteristics of Internet access devices.

The customer experience of the new information

Such changes call for increasing trust to be placed by customers in the services they are accessing: trust in their content and operation, and trust that neither the increased personal information committed to the service, nor the consumer's own dramatically increased accessibility, will be abused. In response to this, a matching redesign of the underlying service and its organisation is required.

In the primarily dial-up environment of the Commoditised Internet, the majority of information and services were largely 'Granular' in nature, the onus being on customers to identify, assess and combine the materials they needed. We looked at this challenge to customer value in some detail in 'Meaning, Trust and Value'.

One step beyond this reorganises the service to match the customer's 'Purposive' mode when they access the service; information is organised so as to correspond with the required tasks. This step alone is a major enhancement, but lacks the full empowerment that the next step in restructuring, 'Decision Support', will bring. This will build on purposive organisation to support customer decisions and enable trust through the provision of an integrated stream of expertise, expert systems and validation services, and it extends this support to the enabling of customer-side collaborative and trading systems.

Finally, matching the move to pervasive access, continuous information will feed between service and appliance, creating the

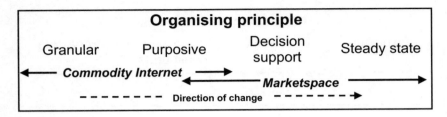

Fig. 11.2 Changing patterns of information organisation.

'Steady State' of operation that allows for automated activities to be carried out without customer intervention. Such streams will generally only be accessed indirectly, through interfaces that allow control of availability and the setting of thresholds and triggers (Fig. 11.2).

KEY POINT

These changes, coupled with the underlying rationalisation of data driven by the sector-specific ontologies we remarked on in Chapter 8, and increasing peer interaction, will affect the nature of customer relationships more profoundly than any other. They introduce a quantum leap in the utility of digital media, and at the same time reduce the customer's workload at the interface, often eliminating all but a selection and configuration stage, after which many key processes are handled automatically.

Putting it together

Bringing these two major dimensions of change together allows us to project some of the types of application that are made possible, and their likely value to the customer. Figure 11.3 explores these characteristics.

Each box in Fig. 11.3 contains a very brief outline of the type of service the combination enables. All such service builds progressively on the basic commoditised Internet and e-commerce sites that are the customary product of providing granular information in fixed-link dial-up environments. The key needs further elaboration.

Boxes shaded with horizontal lines indicate relatively low customer perception of value. We have been exploring the reasons for this in respect of Commoditised

Access characteristics	Granular	Purposive	Decision support	Steady-state
Pervasive	N/A	Component of task specific dedicated appliance	Full automation of some background tasks & part-automated decision support	Customer-independent automated monitoring
Selective continuous	Continuous-access commodity services	Continuous-task support	Support enhanced by part-automated, triggered systems	Switchable automatic monitoring
Ubiquitous	On-demand location-specific services	Just-in-time access to task support	Full range of customer needs addressable on-demand	Background automation with later notification
Fixed-link	Commoditised Internet sites & e-commerce catalogues	Provision of intermittent task support	Addresses customer concern directly, accessibility-dependent	Background automation enabled, intervention denied

Organising principle

Key to customer value perception

Low & device embedded	Medium-value customer support	High-value, declining with familiarity	Sustainable high-value, high-visibility services	High-value, low-visibility background activity

Fig. 11.3 The convenience value map: services enabled by meeting accessibility characteristics with appropriately organised information resources.

Internet services in detail throughout this book. The relatively low value of dedicated task-specific appliances (such as 'smart' refrigerators that monitor their content) arises because, once the novelty wears off, most dedicated devices do not, on their own, appear to do much more than existing systems, such as burglar alarms, already do.

Boxes that are shaded with dots denote services of higher perceived value, the increase being attributable either to improved access so that orders, for instance, can be placed as the need arises, or to improved support for customer tasks.

Boxes with no shading mark services that initially have high perceived value, because the capabilities implemented constitute highly marketable features of appliances or broader digital services. This value declines over time as new features supersede the

SIMPLE LOCATION-BASED SERVICES

It is true that the ability of cellular mobile appliances to identify their user's location enables a range of services that would otherwise be impossible. However, the initial excitement surrounding simple location-based services such as the provision of local timetables and location-specific marketing, may prove to be short-lived. For the most part these will rapidly prove to be threshold functions whose presence is expected with the basic package, not the high-value features that are often anticipated and, as always, the devaluation will be accelerated by inappropriate marketing intruding into the customer task generated, in this case, by local businesses.

KEY POINT

The highest perceived customer value is provided by services of the type suggested in the boxes shaded with diagonal lines. Here information and its organisation generates services that have sustainable value in always-on environments. Sustainable because customer concerns are addressed with comprehensive, contiguous solutions.

old ones, which become threshold functions of the service, 'the least the customer can expect'. An example of this is provided by location-based services such as the provision of local weather or timetables.

The automated services in the light grey boxes may generate the highest real value for both the customer and the business, but conscious value perception will be lower because most of the action takes place 'invisibly' in the background.

HOW TODAY'S BUSINESS MODELS WILL COPE (OR NOT ...)

Having examined some of the sources of value in the developing digital environment, it remains for us to restate the

new paradigm and explore its relationship to some familiar Internet business
models.

We can compare the value proposition of marketspaces with that of the
familiar broad horizontal portals (like
Yahoo!) by positioning them both in this
convenience value map. This also allows
us to speculate on the degree of freedom
that such portals have to exploit the developing opportunities and the barriers
they might face. Figure 11.4 shows their
relative positioning in the value space
we have defined.

KEY POINT

*The marketspace paradigm places
the business opportunity at the
point where services that address
specific domains of customer concern with systematised information, support for decisions and
extensive automation, meet the improved access characteristics offered
by always-on and mobile devices.*

It is immediately clear that, not only are horizontal portals
positioned in direct opposition to marketspaces in respect of

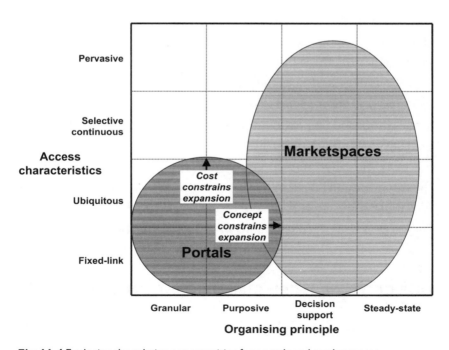

Fig. 11.4 Exploring the relative opportunities for portals and marketspaces.

their value proposition, but also, as the diagram illustrates, they are constrained from expanding far into the higher-value services.

Making all their content and existing services usefully accessible in selective continuous channels would require re-organising them for this usage to render them relevant to particular task sets for which the customer requires support. Expansion in this direction is therefore plausible but expensive, and reference to our value map will show that the majority of the services easily added are of relatively low perceived value.

Providing sustained decision support for key customer domains of concern is equally possible for a portal, and arguably many already do this to a limited degree, but extensive support for a particular domain undermines the horizontal portal concept. Any expansion in this direction must necessarily be modest and balanced.[2]

If portals are unlikely candidates to provide the new services, which of the current Internet business models has the best chance of making the transition? We will shortly extend our review to include three other common basic models: Internet retailers or 'e-tailers', services that aggregate information and products in vertical market sectors (sometimes called 'vortals'), and sites already focused on particular domains of customer concern – support services and communities.

On the convenience value map that we have used above, these three in fact occupy very similar positions. We can only differentiate their central propositions by re-introducing our third customer value dimension, *depth of support for the domain of concern*.

OUR CRITICAL THIRD DIMENSION: COMPLETENESS

The characteristics of the third dimension of value, depth of sup-

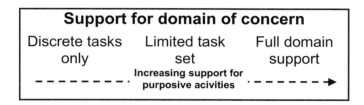

Fig. 11.5 Degrees of support for domain of concern.

port for customer concern, have been explored in detail in earlier chapters and we will use a simple set of distinctions to define them, as shown in Fig. 11.5.

Introducing this dimension we can build a 'Value Cube' that resembles the original Revenue Cube but this time focused entirely on customer value (Fig. 11.6).

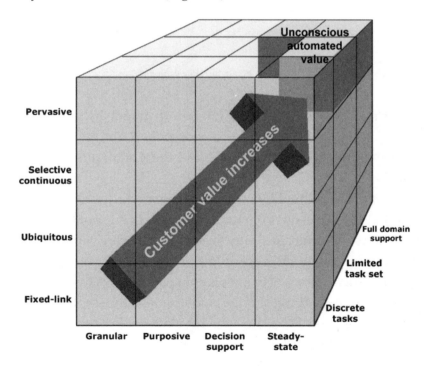

Fig. 11.6 The Value Cube, showing how value for the customer increases towards the top right-hand corner (but also that services in the extreme corner, being automated, are largely executed without the customer's involvement).

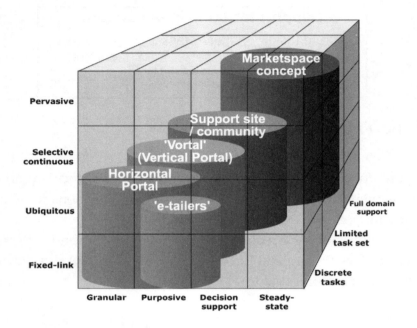

Fig. 11.7 Using the Value Cube to distinguish key value propositions.

Using the Value Cube, we can now distinguish the core value propositions of the model types we described, and compare them with those of horizontal portals and the putative marketspace (Fig. 11.7).

Figure 11.7 should, however, be interpreted with some caution. It does not set out to cover all the types of information or task that each service satisfies, only to establish the core value proposition. It also already allows for some provision of the mobile access that most of these services are planning to provide. Conversely, it does not reflect changes to the underlying business design, that may be triggered by seizing the new opportunities, and which might enable them to shift the value proposition.

Many of these models are less constrained than portals in the new paradigm. Vortals such as Expedia, support sites such as Baxter Renal, and communities, such as iVillage or WebMD, are predicated on more of the value features than less focused services and seem consequently better placed to profit from the new paradigm.

So who will make the transition successfully?

Communities

The support and community-based businesses appear best placed to take advantage of the developing opportunities, but this may prove more difficult than it appears. Most need to make the transition from one of two current forms; either a business support service funded by the vendor (i.e. an extension to the company's marketing) or an advertiser-supported community of interest. The step from there, to a service to which customers would be willing to entrust important concerns and pay for their handling, is not an easy one. In part this is because while elements of the macro-framework for trust may be present, others such as trust in transaction handling will be missing, and the micro-framework of trustpoints will be almost entirely absent.

For communities the problems run deeper. They tend to be founded on a range of conceptions that will obstruct an easy transition:

- They perceive themselves primarily in the publishing mould, reaching out to defined socio-demographic groups and, while their underlying conception of their audiences' needs brings more meaning to the material than is the case with less targeted ventures, the concerns grouped under the umbrella of the service are often only tenuously related;
- A publishing model that depends on advertising revenue for support inevitably pushes them to equate volume with value and overwhelm any task-based features of the service with entertainment, news and audience-building features;

- Conversely, the audience perception of most communities as a variety of focused magazine with participative features, means that they generally view the service as operating at one remove from the goods and services that meet their needs;
- More fundamentally, although there is usually a philosophy of cost recovery, many community services have an underlying not-for-profit ethos, creating a mandate that may embody hard-to-resolve tensions between a benevolent service and a profit-maximising one. Paradoxically, especially where the service is important and their level of personal concern high, customers may value a moderately costly service over a free one.

e-tailers

The dilemma faced by e-tailers is especially interesting. One, extensively adopted, expansion strategy is to use 'brand permission' to extend the product range into adjacent categories, yet this largely precludes the provision of extensive domain support and reinforces the current model, stranding them within the Commoditised Internet. The alternative, extending the range and provision of domain support outside the simple selection/transaction/fulfilment model, might gradually move the proposition higher up the customer value curve; but, as we have pointed out elsewhere, such changes look to retailers, initially at least, like just increasing cost of sales.

'Vortals'

The vertical portals may have more work to do than community sites to extend their value features, but many of them are already developing in the appropriate direction and the commercial relationship is more conducive to their success. Having, as many of them do, a clear focus committed to a distinct customer need and increasingly differentiated by their service features, these businesses are the most obvious existing players to capitalise on the new value paradigm. Having said that, within the consumer market the majority of concerns that might support a marketspace are not coherently addressed by any existing 'vortal'.

Similar observations apply to business-to-business service. As simple, transaction-based services give way to 'business support services' and add supporting features such as brokerage and hedging facilities or business process integration, they also need to improve their access characteristics. Together these additional services move them much closer to the real locus of added value, focusing as they do on client concerns and support for decisions about business risk and limiting exposure.

In practice many major opportunities in business markets lie in providing marketspace patterns of support for business skills and processes, in a fashion that integrates with their execution and operation.

A CALL TO ACTION

We believe that the developing digital environment offers the opportunities and benefits that early pioneers of the medium envisaged. However, to take advantage of these, companies will need to radically adjust both their approach to service provision and in many cases their attitude to partnering and competition.

One factor should concentrate the mind. In addition to retaining one or two portals for basic search services and a selection of entertainment services, customers will almost certainly only ever get to the commitment stage with between five and eight of these services. One or two perhaps to support work or professional development, three or four to support essential financial and domestic management tasks, and one or two in respect of hobbies and interests.

This still leaves room for hundreds of specialised and differentiated services and therefore does not support a renewed case for first-mover advantage being critical as, it has been argued, is the case for developments in the Commoditised Internet. It does however imply a necessity for early and flexible experimentation, to test and absorb the dynamics and to start climbing what is likely to be a steep learning curve. Success will go to the best-organised and most complete service; taking customers who have reached the commitment stage from competitive services is likely to prove very tough.

TO SUMMARISE

- The dynamic relationship between accessibility and information creates a range of new service opportunities that market-spaces are ideally positioned to exploit.
- Not all the new service opportunities will have the same per-ceived value for customers and some are invisible in everyday operation, making them literally 'out-of-sight, out-of-mind'; suppliers of these services may need to associate themselves with others having more recognisably value.
- Among today's well-known business models, portals and e-tailers are both restricted from taking full advantage of new opportunities by limitations of cost and concept.
- Of existing Internet services, 'vortals', support sites aimed at areas of acute customer concern, and some communities, look best placed to benefit and to move into the full marketspace opportunity.
- Businesses wanting to participate in the extended-services revolution need to start experimenting and learning early. Late entrants will find poaching committed customers from estab-lished marketspaces difficult indeed.

THE END OF THE BOOK

Tempting though it is to look for a punchy sting in the tail to finish this book, we've decided upon a rather dryer final: a recap of our key arguments.

What we can briefly say, before closing, is that we believe we have demonstrated conclusively that the successful evolution of the valuable, sustainable digital businesses of the future, will be determined primarily by their willingness to place the requirements of our promiscuous customer at the heart of their offerings.

It is terribly easy to mistake this imperative for an old marketing truism. But hopefully you now share our view, that the deep complexity and very high cost that will feature in the future development of such genuine customer-centric offerings, consign ill-considered or opportunistic approaches to the past.

From here on, an obsessive and exclusive focus on the provision of real value to customers is the rule in digital markets, and modally-based approaches will we hope, be adopted as essential tools.

So, thanks for reading our book, and good luck!

Telling you what we've told you ... again

The blind alley of operational efficiency

Strategy based on endless improvements to operational efficiency and economies of scale reaches a logical point of diminishing returns.[3] Competing on this basis in digital markets leads to a focus on transaction cost reduction and this coupled with price transparency, impacts product marketing in a fashion that rapidly restricts the strategic options; once transaction cost reduction has run its course further competitive price reductions impact margins.

The stripping of sustainable advantage

In digital media at the time of writing, this end-game is in many instances the starting point. Cost leadership, and enormous scale and reach, are entry-level qualifications in digital markets for commodity products, and since customers' switching costs are low, this offers only limited sustainable advantage. Even luxury goods enter digital markets as commodity items when a product marketing approach is adopted. (Most apparent exceptions to this rule turn out to have a focus strategy and substantial service elements within their offer that sustain their position.)

The endless race for differentiation

For product marketers, differentiation in digital media is hard both to achieve and to sustain. Innovation moves so fast that today's unique feature is tomorrow's threshold attribute, or worse just irrelevant. Existing differentiating features are hard to convey emotively or justify in terms of the customer's need, in the sterile and cold environment of the Internet, and are therefore eroded, even ignored, in favour of cheaper generic substitutes. Fundamentally, the product marketing approach fails to leverage the real strengths of digital media, connection, information and information-based services in other than a minimal fashion.

The erosive effect of misplaced marketing strategies

Just as more-of-the-same in optimising efficiency now offers little scope for competitive advantage, marketing and its current partner CRM quickly reach the same condition in digital markets. In this context, CRM's core problem is exposed: the underlying driver is not in fact the customer's benefit, but product sales. The interruptive nature of many loyalty campaigns, the common abuse of customer data that accompanies them – and more importantly the distraction of focus away from real value-building activity – leads to erosion rather than growth of loyalty.

The out-of-control brand

That other pillar of marketing strategy, brand-building, proves in these environments to be more about the satisfaction of the customer's need to perform the essential minutiae of tasks, than about corporate ID and 'lifestyle association', making it hard for lifestyle branding to add value. And the brand is both out of the owner's control much of the time and, literally invisible in many of the most valuable, automated services.

The war on meaning

Part of the product marketer's problem lies in the fact that customers 'need products only when they need them' or when a sense of need is artificially induced. But the scope for massaging need on the Internet and related channels is far lower than it once appeared. The lack of context, in which the majority of digital marketing appears, creates a real crisis of 'lack of meaning' and connections with customer need are hard to make. As a result most marketing communication in digital services merely further frustrates customer purpose, without creating the associations that could drive sales.

A new look at trust

Trust is essential to customer engagement, and in a transparent market, where with a little extra effort the customer can check the features and prices of all the available products, denying immediate access to the full range erodes that trust. Perceived neutrality of the service is thus essential and the product marketer needs to recognise that in most instances in digital markets, they must accept conditions where they appear alongside all their competitors.

The answer lies in Modal Analysis

A way out of this impasse lies in 'true customer-centric thinking', meeting the need in digital markets for the information that underpins all decision making and much necessary activity in day-to-day life. This approach demands the development of services that meet the customer's need to perform purposive activities in pursuit of identifiable goals, simplifying rather than complicating their lives, and leading to a progressive cycle of engagement.

The new paradigm of the marketspace

The creation of 'marketspaces' focused on customer concerns or interests, rather than on market segments, and encompassing the entire 'value space' surrounding the subject matter, allows valuable, information-based services predicated on fulfilling the customer's purpose, to become the primary proposition and source of revenue. For product marketers, a bonus of this approach is that products that are relevant in such spaces have real context-driven value connected to real customer needs and are thus less commodity items than necessary components of the transient value chain that meets the immediate purpose.

Information finds its place in digital markets

Some service features, such as personalised newsletters, are already integral to many digital offers. And services that build customer return visits such as on-line diaries, portfolio management and storage facilities are provided in a range of contexts. But they are generally free or a commodity feature of product- or advertising-driven markets, not the core of the offer. The advent of always-on mobile connectivity and pervasive services has changed that. The customer is now within reach to receive just-in-time information and support when time-sensitive decisions are needed. Now, context-specific clusters of information-based services are not only achievable, they can automate critical task sets, making them the key to competitive advantage.

Loyalty revisited

Support for day-to-day tasks in pursuit of the customer's purposive engagement by both managing and simplifying essentials, and by engaging with their interests, offers real sustainable advantage. Customers do not so much adopt as annex such services, building them into the fabric of their lives, creating not loyalty but commitment. Switching costs are suddenly genuinely high, and since the customers configure many services themselves and the complex of delivery capabilities are unique, the scope for imitation by competitors is limited. This is where customer relationships are really built in a digital environment.

NOTES

1   Clayton M. Christiansen, *The Innovator's Dilemma: When New Technologies Cause Great Firms to Fail*, Harvard Business School Press, 1997.
2   Because portals are constrained from this kind of expansion, we should not conclude that they will be superseded by the new models. In their function as navigators, key directories of available resources, they will retain a central role.
3   Gary Hamel, *Leading the Revolution*, Harvard Business School Press, 2000.

Index